SPARK and Inspire

30 DAYS OF MEANINGFUL INSIGHT TO SPARK YOUR BUSINESS AND INSPIRE YOUR SOUL

ROBIN Norgren

©2012 Robin Norgren All Rights Reserved

Introduction:

The quest to run a successful business seems at first glance something you have to take on solo. And at the beginning that might need to happen. The details of how your vision comes forth has to be done in the heart first and then, once you take the leap, you can bring in trusted guides to cheer you on, give you straight talk, share in the burden of the hard work and the uncertainties.

Sometimes, you may not have a community of people around you who are passionate about a vision, have no desire to jump into the deep end and create a business. And for a time this will be OK. Again it helps to challenge how high your commitment level is for this idea you may have been kicking around for awhile.

But...

When you have finally set your course

Or...

When you have been smack dab in the middle of this idea of yours and really want to hear from those who have felt the victories and the disappointments of taking such a brave leap, community and inside advice with no expectations or strings attached... well you need it.

Within these pages you will find the voices of over 40 creative entrepreneurs who run their businesses both online and in brick and mortar stores, who run workshops and sell in shows, who have a range of experiences and have been in business from 1 year to more than 25 years and who offer you no nonsense information on their processes and how they have been able to keep moving in tough economic times and how they have found a way to let good ideas go when the money was not in line with the dream. We are talking on a range of topics from collaborations to big leaps that did (and did not) come together as planned. We are talking about how to get at the soul of your business and how to stay excited about the work you offer the world.

30 days worth of questions that you can take and use as a 30 day diagnostic for your idea, vision or business.

QUESTION #1
Collaborations: a good idea?

Every journey starts with a separation, a leave-taking, a realization that the place you are right now is a place where you can no longer stay.

Justine Musk

In 2011, it seemed that everything I was creating was a collaborative effort. I lived outside of the United States for the majority of 2010. So when I arrived home I found myself saying YES TO ANYTHING my friends were working on in an effort to reconnect.

I created and executed a preschool program for a small start up church. I co-facilitated a support group for women called "Mending the Soul." I illustrated my first children's book with a friend. None of them went well. In fact, these friendships still feel strained to this day (I actually wrote a 4 week course on collaboration as a result of this experience!).

You have heard it said that it is best NOT TO work with friends. And for a while after these experiences I would have said AMEN to that. But today I think that I would try again but I would take what I have learned from those past collaborations and walk into future ones more wisely.

Here is what I know:

-the power structure of the collaboration must be firmly established. None of the tasks can be ambiguously left for someone to organically decide who is responsible for them.

-if monetary investments are involved, KNOW that the one with the money holds the power; it is no longer collaboration.

-decide IN ADVANCE whose ass is on the line is something doesn't get done. Taking ownership and responsibility ESPECIALLY for the main parts of the project are MANDATORY

-DECIDE UP FRONT what the non-negotiables are for the project for each party involved and THEN DECIDE if it is a good idea to go forward.
With these four keys fleshed out beforehand, I think that even friends can work together with minimal strain on the relationship.

Kelly Thiel:
I do think that collaborations are a good idea. Sometimes when two artists get together, a beautiful synergy is created. Ideas just flow and wonderful things can happen. It's also a great way to reach out to other audiences that you may not normally interact with. I would say that a blog hop is a sort of collaboration, just an online one with many contributing artists!

My favorite type of collaboration though, is when two artists in different mediums get together to create a single (or multiple!) piece(s) of art. Integrating both mediums and working off each other's design, the two artists come together to create one finished piece.

Jan Avellana:

Yes, I think collaborations have the potential to further relationships between artists as well as help promote both our own artwork, and the artwork of our fellow artists. The trick, I think, is to find a right fit, someone who shares our values, our aesthetic or at the very least, someone who we feel we can work with in a give and take fashion. As yet, I haven't worked on any truly collaborative projects, but I certainly look forward to it in the future!

Nolwenn Petitbois:

I have never done a collaborative piece of art yet. But it is something that crosses my mind from time to time when I see amazing artwork by other artists that decided to jump and collaborate with someone else.
However, I have created collaborative art journals via Round Robins and got mixed emotions with it. Some pages got lost; some entire journals were never received... I guess this is something that can happen unfortunately. Over all, it was a nice thing to receive pages from different people from all over the World, in styles sometimes far from mine which is very interesting as well.

Collaboration can be scary if you don't know the other artist well, if you don't have the same view of what the final piece should be. BUT it is also something very exciting knowing that another artist will add his/her own personal touch and then release it to the world with you. And I think it is a good idea as it offers the possibility of receiving more exposure thanks to the artists with whom you collaborate. It can bring new customers that may not have known about you otherwise.

Kelly Warren:

My experience with collaborations has been fairly limited, and I'm not sure the experience I did have would be considered a true collaboration, but I'll share it and let you decide!

In 2008, I did a large Fat Book Swap. There were ten women involved and ten themes. The idea was to create 10 cards of each theme (basically the same 4 x 4 card 10 times), meaning we each created 100 total 4 x 4 cards. We then sent everything to the person doing the organizing, the wonderful Roni (http://inkstainswithroni.blogspot.com/). I was amazed at how quickly Roni gathered each participant's work and sent us out back out a 100-card package of wonderfulness! I had a special box custom crafted to keep my full set in and enjoy looking back through them often.

This collaboration was a challenge for me as I'd just gotten started in mixed media, but it really pushed me to try new things and I found that I really enjoyed the 4 x 4 format. The deadlines pushed me a little bit, but only having to come up with one design for each theme (even though I had to create 10 of each design) helped some. Would I do it again? Absolutely. I learned tons of new techniques, made some great blog friends, and have a beautiful box chock full of 100 pieces of original art to show for it! You can see my entries in the collaboration at this link:
http://happyshackdesigns.blogspot.com/search?q=Fat+Book+Entry&max-results=20&by-date=true

Alease McClenningham:

Collaboration is the best idea for those wanting to reach a wider audience. I strongly believe that when you start out in any type of business it is to vital to seek out others who like your work and are familiar with you as a person. Friends and family are the best people to start with in the collaboration process because they will spread the word about your business, which will then be shared with other liked minded people.

Jean Simrose:

Collaboration: working with someone to produce or create something; partnership; joint intellectual effort; to cooperate.
I am collaborative by nature. Being an extrovert I solidify new ideas for my jewelry business by talking to other people. Making connections with people, coming up with ideas, bringing variety to my work are all positives for me. I enjoy the company of others and sometimes need the challenge they bring to express my creativity fully and gain confidence in my work.

So far I have taken new classes to satisfy my need to collaborate. One of my goals is to find a "group" that I fit in where I have similar-minded people to collaborate with. I am always looking for ways to improve my work and connect with others. My jewelry business depends on it to succeed. People have to like the jewelry I create in order to want to buy it!

Leanne Wargowsky:

"If civilization is to survive, we must cultivate the science of human relationships - the ability of all peoples, of all kinds, to live together, in the same world at peace." - Franklin D. Roosevelt.

And so my belief goes . . . are collaborations a good idea? Most definitely YES! From music (Lennon& McCartney) to dancing (Astaire& Rogers), ice cream (Ben & Jerry) to computers (Hewlett & Packard), the list of amazingly successful collaborations is long and wide. I am a strong believer of strength in numbers, and any time two creative souls gather . . . I am certain great things will come of it. My most successful creative endeavors have been born out of idea bouncing and feedback that I have received from another. Setting responsibilities and boundaries are so important in the process. But once established, the sky is the limit. Anyone interested in collaborating? Call me! ;)

Sonya McCllough:

I have been blessed with the ability to generate some awesome ideas through prayer. Ideas are abundantly mine. Just for the asking. Conceptual thinking is my gift. The ability to get a project done is also a gift I have been blessed with. While not considering an all important detail is my greatest weakness. This is why I love Collaborations. When women collaborate, they simply get more done and get more done efficiently.

YOUR TURN:
Collaborations: a good idea?

QUESTION #2
Success in business is defined as....

"When we are enthusiastic we are intoxicated with passion rooted in our true selves and it flows into all we do."

Linda Saccoccio

For the first couple of years of my online business I wanted so much to really make all the money that people seemed to allude to. More marketing, more connecting, constant blogging, relisting on etsy, social media at all hours of the day and night. Oh! And make sure you are near your email just in case that huge wholesale order comes in...

After months and months of questioning my work ethic (maybe I was not committed enough) and my pricing structure (are my prices too high?), I finally stopped. I had to take a good hard look at the reality: the business was running me.

I had to admit that I felt this pressure ALL THE TIME about this business which at best was making a supplemental income for the hours of labor I was putting into it. Here are some things that helped me to redefine my definition of success:

1. I began logging EXACTLY how much time I was spending in each area of my business and correlating that with sales

2. I got REAL about my accounting for my business.

3. I took a break for about 30 days where I created NOTHING.

Today I define success in business as:
The ability to be able to create what I love in a manner that inspires me and thus flows into the quality and design of my products and feeds not just my pocketbook but my soul.

Nolwenn Petitbois:

Success in business, for me, is defined as being able to be recognized as being an artist both by my peers AND by myself.

Success in business is having happy customers that come back and order something else and talk positively about you and what you do.

Jan Avellana:

Hmmm...I'd say that I define "success in business" as reaching your financial goals in a way that comfortably sustains the business, while engaging in meaningful work that is aligned with your personal values and goals. "Success in business" also means growing your business at a rate that allows you to maintain your sanity and avoids burnout.

As indie artists, so many times we wear all of the hats and play all of the important business roles from accountant to marketing specialist to artist, so having a successful business also means having enough down time to just be a normal human-being instead of having to work around the clock to get it all done.

Sonya McCllough:

Success in business to me is defined as my life (offline & online) & my business both reflect a single objective which is to inspire others with words & images.

Jean Simrose:

Success in business for me is being financially secure while I'm doing something I love. I need to feel like I'm appreciated and that I inspire others. Art and crafts have always been a way for me to connect with people.

When I worked as a mental health social worker I facilitated a support group for my clients to teach them ways to relax. I taught them different art projects; I watched them express themselves creatively and become passionate about something. It gave me a sense of accomplishment in my work.

Unfortunately working in the mental health field is very stressful in other ways and causes a lot of social workers to "burn out". Before I did that I decided to pursue other avenues to get what I needed to feel successful. I want to be sought after for my jewelry, to be respected in the industry and be inspired and feel fulfilled by my work. I also need to feel as though I am contributing in some small way and teaching others helps me to do that. I have a long way to go to accomplish my goals but I'm enjoying the journey!

Alease M. McClenningham:

A business that showcases your true love. And you are happy working, managing and growing the business.

Kelly Thiel:

I've recently been able to narrow down my definition of success a bit more. It used to be something akin to "Make Cool Stuff". Not so much anymore. Now that I have two young daughters, I am interested in generating income to use for the education of these two girls. I have recently decided that I will be "successful" if I can do several things: Generate enough money with my art for the 'education fund', exhibit with a certain caliber of galleries, and receive some peer recognition. The thought of these things keeps me awake some nights. But I think that's a good thing 😊

Leanne Wargowsky:

I'd love to say that success in business has only to do with following your dreams and nothing to do with maintaining financial independence while doing it . . . but I wouldn't be honest saying that. In a perfect world; I would be able to sit in a studio from sun up to sun down, painting my heart away, as little blue birds flew in and out of my house, tending to the dishes, laundry and children. Of course, money would grow on the trees outside of my little studio and I would simply GIVE my art away to the hundreds lined up outside my door, as "selling" would be of no concern.

However, life is not always perfect. So, to my realistic creative soul, success in business is being true to my artistic thoughts and ideas, being able to produce and create my work, and selling my art to others in a manner that will offer greater financial stability to my family and me. All while maintaining a healthy balance between my life and my art. That, to me, would be success.

Stephanie Amos:

I've been pondering how to end this statement for days. And what I have concluded is that my own personal success in business is defined by customer satisfaction and my own contentment with the creativeness that I have shared.

Let me explain: If we don't care about our customer's happiness, then why are we in business? I'm a people pleaser by nature anyways, so it only makes sense that this idea carries over while selling my work. This concept helps me to strive for excellence in creating my art and in working with my clients.

I also mentioned that my own satisfaction is also important to the success of my own personal business. I believe that if you're not happy with the art you have created, it will reflect in how you present the piece. For example, if I created a painting that I absolutely love, it will show in how I present it to people. My enthusiasm will shine through and others may also find the piece intriguing. But if I created a painting that I really didn't care for, that feeling would carry on with that piece as well, making it more difficult for me to sell because I don't even like it, and so why would someone else?

Kelly Warren:

I think this is a very interesting topic, and I think it all depends on your goals and your outlook. For me, my art business is not my main source of income.

I have a pretty demanding full-time career in higher education on top of my art. So for me, success in my art business is simply finding the time to put a little bit of me out into the world for others to enjoy.

Would I love to be able to "quit the day job" and devote more time to my art? Absolutely, but I know that's simply not a possible reality at this point in my life. So maybe for me, success in business is defined as knowing what my limitations are (time!) and embracing them rather than fighting them. Fighting them takes an awful lot of energy that could be better spent on enjoying the process instead.

YOUR TURN:

Success in business is defined as....

Question #3
THE HARDEST PART ABOUT PURSUING A DREAM IS . . .

Owning our story and loving ourselves through that process is the bravest thing we will ever do.

Brene Brown

the tenacity, the determination, the drive, the risk, the stamina, the hard work, the long days, the sleepless nights, the loneliness, the uncertainty, the confusion, the discouragement, the frustration, the spirit draining, the fatigue, the unknown.

And yet... something inside me cannot let go of dreaming. It reminds me of hope and without hope what is the point of living?

NOLWENN PETITBOIS:

never giving up. But with time, and no matter how big or how small the dream is, I realized that giving up was the easiest way out. The best way not to be disappointed is to actually never get near the point we wanted to arrive to. But what if the dreamers were true when saying that the harder you work the greater the reward?

I believe that a dream can't end up in your life if you did nothing for it, absolutely nothing for it.

I may be wrong but this is how I see it, for me anyway.

Another very hard part about pursuing a dream is the trust issue. Feeling in your gut that no matter how your dream will come true, it WILL come true for sure. Sometimes, we envision a whole big map to go from the dream's seed to the dream in full bloom, set up a timeline even.

But once you trust and commit to go on despite the bumps on the roads,
each and every dream can come true.

Jean Simrose:

My dream has been an ever-changing challenge throughout my life. I am interested in so many things that my focus has continually changed over the years. I have been a licensed beautician, done accounting, worked for an oil company and worked as a mental health social worker. Creating things and working with my hands has always been a hobby. Making a career of it has been the hardest part of pursuing this dream. I sometimes question my talent and ability to make jewelry people will buy. I internalize the negativity from others who don't believe I can succeed. It is difficult not to become disillusioned in my own ability to follow my dreams.

Surrounding myself with supportive, positive people who believe in me helps me to follow my ultimate dream….creating things that people value and inspiring others to follow their dreams as well.

Alease McClenningham:

. . . the naysayers.

There are so many people who are non-believers that they can derail your dreams.

The important thing is to only listen to yourself and your needs.

It is important to surround yourself with positive people.

Kelly Warren:

I think the hardest part about pursuing a dream, first and foremost, is taking that first step and putting it out there! And then the second hardest part about pursuing that dream is remaining realistic about your situation and what's doable at whatever point you are in your life.

That means accepting that the dream may not happen tomorrow, or the next day, or the next month, or even the next year. But as long as you keep it out there and keep trying, even if it's just inch by inch, hope springs eternal.

That said, I think another aspect of that, which sticks with the reality theme, is accepting when you need to take a step back and reevaluate. One of my dreams is to have a retreat center and offer art retreats. I found the perfect spot a couple years ago…if only I had 1.3 million dollars lying around! So that's when I had to reevaluate! I've still moved forward with facilitating art retreats, but I had to reevaluate and figure out how I could make it happen on a smaller scale, and that's when Mermaids and Mamas Artful Adventure was born: Purple Cottage Retreats. I still haven't given up on the big dream, just seeing what I can do in the meantime to get me there.

Jan Avellana:

Having a vision of what you want to do, and where you want to go, but being unable to pursue it wholeheartedly. Pursuing a dream is also difficult because often, this pursuit entails sacrifice—money, time, emotion—and these sacrifices may affect the people you live with, who depend on you to be fully present for them and to provide financially for them. Sometimes pursuing my artistic dreams feels too foolish, the price, too high to pay, considering everyone involved. I am finding in my own creative journey, that in order to pursue my creative dreams, I must also find a way to supplement my earnings with an outside job—a challenge to be sure, with two young children and a Hawaii-sized mortgage!

Sonya McCllough:

holding tight to the whisper of the dream.

The soft and delicate whisper is much like the wind.
Only felt ... never seen or heard by any other then the dreamer herself.

Stephanie Amos:

listening to your heart and ignoring everyone else who thinks you should be doing something different with your life, including yourself. I believe I have finally realized that I am an artist and creating art is what I should be doing with my life. I can't tell you how much of a burden has been lifted from my shoulders in knowing that I am blessed with the opportunity to pursue my dream now.

Now all I need to do is move forward with
ACCEPTANCE   COURAGE   and   CONFIDENCE!

Kelly Thiel:

all the evil demons whispering in your ears about doubting yourself and your art. And then, there are the nay-sayers in your circle of friends and family, and they don't always give you the strength and support you need. Sometimes you feel awfully alone, and it is wonderful if you can find a friend who shares your entrepreneurial spirit.

The other challenge for me is the balance. I have a baby and a preschooler, so my attention is divided between my family and my business. Some days, I feel super motivated to work, but then I am needed elsewhere. I want to be present in my time with my girls, but thoughts of work often creep in, if I'm not careful. To be successful in work and in motherhood is a constant juggling act for me.

YOUR TURN:

THE HARDEST PART ABOUT PURSUING A DREAM IS . . .

Question #4

The hardest part at year 2 of your business is....

"The more resistance you experience, the more important your unmanifested art/project/enterprise is to you - and the more gratification you will feel when you finally do it."

-

Steven Pressfield, The War of Art

The newness of the business and the excitement of all that could be in your new little bundle of joy really wraps a little cocoon around you and protects you from the rough spots and the tons of work that goes on in year 1. You really live on adrenalin and hope and ooey gooey dreams...

Year 2 really grabs you and makes you pay attention to what is and IS NOT working in your business. IN year 2 you really are paying attention as to whether or not your work is going to produce financial results. Year 2 is when you got to get honest about how long you can sustain an all out type of work schedule ESPECIALLY if you are still waiting on break even results. Year 2 truly can offer a 'come to Jesus' moment: is this a business or is this a hobby?

Alease McClenningham:

The hardest part at year 2 of your business is…. for me it has been staying focused. I like to do a lot of things. But I know that the only way to continue to grow my business I have to stay focused on what's working and only add a few ideas at a time.

Leanne Wargowsky:

I'll let you know when I get there. ;-) Yes, if you see my bio, you know that I am a newbie in this creative business life. While I participated in the Kelly Rae Roberts' ecourse called Flying Lessons in 2010, it has taken me a little bit longer to wake up and "smell the coffee". As I slowly approach year two, I imagine the hardest part will be finding balance to create vs. running the business part of things. Even now I find myself struggling with moments when I'd love to just sit and paint and create, but know that there is some *BUSINESS* to tend to. The creating has to take a back seat. And, keeping it all straight on the business end. Yes, I'm fairly certain *THAT* will be my challenge. Time will tell . . .

Nolwenn Petitbois:

I currently am in this year 2 of business, or so. The hardest part right now is to find new ways to market what I have to offer and to have my customers to come back and buy something else.

My testimonials and feedbacks are good, but there seems to be something missing that I still need to figure out. I know I will eventually (figure this out) but sometimes, looking at my shop stats and not getting depressed because of what I see is hard.

I have faith in my artwork, and in the fact that it can touch people. Not everyone for sure, as my style is whimsical and my Nixies are far from looking realistic. But I know there are some women (and men too) that feel empowered by my messages. I just have to find them, or let them find their way to me.

Again, it's about commitment to my business and trust.

Kelly Warren:

Year two for me was in 2007, so this was before the U.S. economy tanked. My girls were going on two years old and I was traveling to about eight juried arts festivals a year. I can't say that the hardest part of year two was growing my business. My business itself was actually doing very well. My shows were very successful. Given that, I think that hardest part of that year for me was actually the growth. I was not at the point that I could (or even was willing, frankly) to "give up the day job" for my creative business. I'm very much a people person, and the interaction I have with those I work with in my day job keeps me young. I work with college students all day!

The greater challenge for me at that point was the juggle: working full-time, being a wife and a mother to two year old twins, AND creating artwork for and running a creative business. To this day, the juggle is still my greatest challenge. I think many creatives at year two might be getting to the point of asking themselves the "Will I be able to quit my day job and devote my time fully to my creative business soon?" question. But I wasn't at that point. I wasn't asking that question because I knew that I wasn't ready for that, mentally or financially.

For me, the most important part of year two, year one, year eight, year twenty, year whatever, is simply knowing yourself and what you truly want out of what you are doing. Am I getting to the point at which I'd feel more comfortable walking away from the day job and devoting my "work-time" fully to my creative business? Maybe now, at year seven...maybe. Yet, I'm a very realistic person and know that the changes that would have to take place to make that happen aren't quite ready to change yet. There are dreams, and I have them, but I also keep a healthy grip on reality. To me, I believe that healthy grip is the most important thing to have when building and growing a creative business.

Sonya McCllough:

The hardest part at year 2 of your business is finally knowing where you would like your business to be in say ... five years. But, knowing it will take time (maybe, even five years) of travel time to reach our true destination.

Jean Simrose:

The hardest part in following my dream is not having sufficient funds to carry out all of my business goals. I envisioned taking more classes, learning more techniques and collaborating with more people. I planned on going to art retreats and connecting with like-minded people who inspire me. Instead I found myself working hard just to participate in fairs and keep my Etsy shop stocked so I could sell my jewelry.

The *MIND. BODY. SOUL ART JOURNALING E-COURSE* has helped me to further defines my dreams. I have learned a lot about what I truly want from my creative business and how to get it. The e-course facilitated this Project. I hope it will lead to more connections in my creative business world.

Kelly Thiel:

Momentum. Keeping the momentum. Life happens. People get sick, and pregnancies occur. It is so hard to stay focused on your business when life keeps throwing distractions at you. And since you are your own boss, it's easy to let things slide a bit. Not always a problem (since sometimes you really do need a break every now and then), but once that period is over, sometimes I find it hard to get going again. I am in amazement at people who never seem to lose momentum. I admire them for their continuous efforts!

At this time in my life when I have two young children at home, I realize that I am going to have to be flexible in my work schedule. There are days when I know I won't be able to put much toward my business. On those days, I try to do ONE THING that will put me one step closer to my goals. It may be something as small as tweeting and Facebooking about an exhibit I'm in, or writing a quick blog post. It may be one business phone call, or even packing a box to ship to a gallery. Just one thing. And then for the rest of the chaotic day, I will know that I haven't lost ALL momentum!

I've also taken to getting up an hour earlier several times a week. It's not much, but it can make a difference to my mental state. I know I've gotten at least a little done for my business before the rest of the household gets up!

Jan Avellana:

...wearing all of the hats. I had great difficulty juggling it all; motherhood, wife, artist, bookkeeper, blogger, social media and marketing guru...at this point in the life of Hazelnut Cottage (my hand stamped jewelry line), I was barely getting any sleep at all and working much of the time. This was especially hard since my babies were little; just 2 and 4 at the time.

YOUR TURN:

The hardest part at year 2 of your business is....

QUESTION #5

What color is your Business?

"I arise in the morning torn between a desire to save the world and a desire to savor the world. This makes it hard to plan the day."

-

E.B. White

I can't believe I am saying this but the color of my business is pink! I am not normally into pink and actually I very rarely wear the color. When I first started my business I gravitated to orange and yellow and all things funky, all things boho. And then suddenly my life, my heart, my business took a feminine turn.
I got more heart centered, more soulful. The business became more about the "why" I do business and why I was just the person to serve those that connect in my business. So here I am embracing who I am... and embracing pink.

Kelly Thiel:

I had to think about this one for about 2 seconds. Then I knew. Pale Yellow. My business is Pale Yellow for several reasons. Right now, I know that my business is a paler version of what it could be. I want it to be a bright, blazing, and cheerful yellow, but right now it isn't. My business is at a slow simmer and hopefully over the next few years as the kids start school, I'll be able to turn up the heat and bring it to a boil. It's an exciting thought and one that keeps me awake at night!

Nolwenn Petitbois:

I would say «Teal». Because running Inner Voices feels like being on a constant wave. Sometimes I crash and burn on the rocks that are put in my way, sometimes I feel like I am on top of the World and can accomplish everything my Heart and Soul desire.
I am swimming in a huge ocean of Creative beings and it is not always easy to find my place, to figure out how to get noticed in all the wonderful art that is created and shared and sold each day.

Jan Avellana:

Right now, my hand stamped jewelry business is in transition in a big way, so I'd have to say that dark grey describes my business at the moment. There are many things I am letting go of, many new things I am venturing towards, but right now I am in the middle of getting from here to there. This is the scary moment of letting go, that moment of leaping before the net appears. All is not lost, since I do believe that the best is yet to be, that's why I've chosen "grey" and not "black"! There is a quote by Anatole France and it reads:

> "All changes, even the most longed for, have their melancholy; for what we leave behind us is a part of ourselves; we must die to one life before we can enter another."

This is what "grey" speaks to me today...

Sonya McCllough:

The color that describes my business these days is **GREY** ... a sweet combination of black & white (which express my view of this world)

Jean Simrose:

I've always had an affinity to turquoise. When I was designing my business cards I decided to use a favorite photograph my husband took of a dragonfly. To make the picture more dramatic we decided to make a color negative of it. The red dragonfly turned out turquoise and the green rosebud turned purple.

Turquoise: represents a higher heart; creative communicators; trusting intuition and femininity.

Purple: represents higher mind power; good judgment; peace of mind and inspiration.

I love these two colors together and they seem to fit with my creative business.

Leanne Wargowsky:

When I first read this question, I thought "easy peesy!" But the more I looked at the color wheel, I felt drawn to so many of the colors out there. Trying to narrow an artistic person down to one color is quite a challenge.

The color RED is represented widely in my studio, as bookshelves and frames and accent pieces here or there. Red gives off a great energy and inspires me to take chances and be BOLD in my work. However, I must choose YELLOW as the main color to describe my business . . . Bright and sunny, and full of creative energy. Yellow is said to stimulate mental processes and encourage communication. Much of my art has to do with inspiring and encouraging, and I can't think of a better way to encourage communication with others.

"Some painters transform the sun into a yellow spot; others transform a yellow spot into the sun." - Pablo Picasso

Kelly Warren:

"I cannot pretend to feel impartial about colors. I rejoice in the brilliant ones and am genuinely sorry for the poor browns." ~ Sir Winston Churchill.

Did you know that Winston Churchill was also an artist? And his quote sums up my love of color. What color describes my business? Bright, happy colors! The name of my business I think clearly reflects my outlook on life and my love of color. When you think of a "happy shack," what color do you picture it to be? I certainly don't think of brown. I think of bright Caribbean blue, with pink porch ceilings and aqua doors.

Every room inside this little shack is painted a different color, each just as happy. And in this, my friends, I have truly described for you what my own home looks like to a T. And that love of color is reflected in my work. My jewelry designs are filled with brightly colored handmade glass beads and gemstones, my photography is juicy with saturated color, and my mixed media work is spilling in color as well. I can't pick a favorite. I love every color on God's beautiful rainbow.

Stephanie Amos:

After putting much thought into this I have concluded that **orange** describes KoiStudios. I have three reasons why. One is that orange is one of my favorite colors. It's such a cheerful color and makes me happy. I would hope that anyone that collects my art is happy when they receive a package from KoiStudios. The second reason is that orange is a warm and inviting color, one that represents me and my business well. The last reason reflects the name of my business, **Koi**Studios. When I think of koi fish, I immediately think of the orange koi first. So naturally, orange is the best color that describes my business!

YOUR TURN:

What color is your Business?

QUESTION #6

In rapid fire fashion, write down 10 words that describe your business. Share your thoughts on these words.

The moment somebody says to me, "This is very risky," is the moment it becomes attractive to me.

- Kate Capshaw

Empowering —to make the decision to take your skills and wisdom off the grid so to speak and find a way to monetize them... well I could even change the word to EXHILARATING!

Frustrating — There are many MANY days strung together — especially with your online work — where you feel like what is the point? Is anyone even listening?

Patient- next to motherhood... OK and MARRIAGE! There has never been anything else that has tested my moxy

Seeds- I feel a momentum building with my brand. Where I started has blossomed into a lovely bushel of ideas which I pray will cultivate into a strong oak tree

Inner Knowing- I think there has got to a strong sense of when you are going in the right direction and when you need to switch gears and that you have separate the emotions from your projects in order to really gauge the direction you need to go

Presence - this piggy backs off inner knowing. I heard about a skill that all great entrepreneurs have in common: the ability to pivot. I think you need presence to do that.

Fulfilled- this is equal parts the hardest thing to be (an entrepreneur) and the most fulfilling. I am addicted.

Joy- coupled with fulfilled. New ideas light me up. Ideas becoming reality set me ON FIRE.

Stamina – you feel me, right? This thing ain't for the weak

Diligence- yep, coupled with stamina FO SHO

Trust- in yourself, in your instincts, in your ability to move forward and let go… oh yeah you need huge amounts of this.

Yep I came up with 11. I was going to edit out the last one but the thought was so strong and I feel like it is closely related to the others so I left it.

Nolwenn Petitbois:

Exciting
Evolving
Inspired
Passionate
Sincere
Heartful
Loved
Thoughtful
Dreamed
Thankful

I put a lot into my business, even in moments when I feel like I don't do enough. Dreams, Gratitude for the good and the bad, Passion, Love... they are all things that I try to stick to... My core values in life.

Jean Simrose:

1. **Creative** – using my imagination to come up with new designs.
2. **Intuition** – following my heart and my feelings to get in-tune with my "inner whispers". (Kelly Rae Roberts)
3. **Inspiration** – getting insight and motivation from others and inspire others with my work.
4. **Contribute** – knowledge and time to others to help inspire them.
5. **Networking** – connecting with other creative people to get inspiration and to grow my business.
6. **Ever-changing** – my goals, my direction, my style.
7. **Personal growth** – business knowledge, marketing skills, defining more effective goals, learning new techniques, connecting with others.
8. **Expand** – my exposure, my product line, my participation in shows.
9. **Satisfaction** – with what I'm doing and how I'm doing it....with soul.
10. **Fulfilling** – to create things people love and teaching others.

Sonya McCllough:

inspired ... by HIM
obedient ... to HIM
biblical ... evidence
love ... evidence
natural ... transition
dependent ... on HIM
crazy ... obedience
clean ... heart
dirty ... is this work
impulsive ... HIS direction often feels

Alease McClenningham:
1. Teachable
2. Basic
3. Creative
4. Social
5. Growing
6. Changing
7. Timely
8. Clients
9. Passionate
10. Stardom

Kelly Warren:

My ten words and what they mean to me:

Happy: This was easily the first thought that popped in my head, and not just because of the name of my business. I know that my business is a "business," but for me, it's also something that just makes me happy. Perhaps not all parts of it make me happy, some parts are certainly more "work" that others, but the simple act of sitting down and creating something, whether it's a piece of jewelry, a new book, or a new series of photos, makes me happy.

Scattered: I think this word describes me in general, so it naturally translates to my business. I have a friend in town who is a very talented painter. She works full-time as I do, but she's able to produce a massive amount of paintings on top of her full-time job. The advice she gave me was to "not be so scattered," and I know she was referring to the variety of media I work in. I thought about that a lot, but then decided that I was okay with being scattered. I like having the ability to sit down and make jewelry one weekend, go on a photography shoot another weekend, and mess around with artist books the next weekend. It may sound crazy, but it works.

Messy: However, scattered definitely leads to messy. Because I work in so many different media, my studio is crammed full of entirely too many supplies and therefore tends to be pretty messy. My studio space is pretty small, so I have boxes of supplies and shipping materials stashed in various places around the house. Not every organized, I realize, but the best I can do at this point! Oh to have a nice, large, open studio space that would hold all my stuff!

Diverse: See "scattered" above. J So I guess the good way to look at "scattered" is that that scatteredness (I think I just made up a word) brings about a diversity of creative work. I participate in our local arts market once a month, rotating between jewelry and photography, and it seems to work well for me. I haven't started selling my artist books yet; I still get too attached to them.

Crowded: See "messy" above! Sometimes I truly can't walk around my space.

Relaxing: You would think that all that scattered, messy craziness would be stressful, but most of the time it's the opposite. When my studio gets to where I can't find anything, I spend some time cleaning up, getting everything back in its place so I can start creating a new mess all over again. That cleanup process is very relaxing for me, as is the process of creating itself. My job can be pretty high stress and the juggle that is my life can also be pretty stressful at times, so my creative time is a great stress reliever.

Fulfilling: Simply put, I love what I do. I've loved creating things, in whatever iteration they've taken at the time, since I was a child. Putting little pieces of me out into the world is very fulfilling.

Challenging: The challenge is in the juggle. I'm long past the point where I could have stopped this crazy train. There comes a point in the growth of a business where you realize, no matter how crazy your world is, you can't turn back now. You've invested too much time and effort and money to stop. That's the challenge. I hit that point about three years ago, so my challenge now is always finding a way to keep all the balls in the air.

Inspirational: When this word popped in my head, I really thought of it in terms of my girls. I've realized that I'm not only an inspiration to them as their Mama, but I'm also an inspiration to them as an artist. I've learn that they tell all their friends and their teachers about my creative business, and they are so proud of me. I just received an email from one of their teachers wishing me well on my recent knee surgery. I asked my girls if they told their teacher about my surgery and they both said, "Mama! Mrs. Morrison reads your blog!" That's when I knew they had been bragging on me. Made me smile.

Me: Lastly, just me. I think my business truly reflects me. My personality (I'm typically a pretty happy girl), my love of color, my love of cars (have you SEEN how many photos I've taken of cars!?), and my love of just "doing." But not doing what everyone else is doing. I don't follow trends. I simply do my own thing. I'm simply me.

Kelly Thiel:

Frustrating - I get so frustrated sometimes, because I cannot work as much as I want to. I want to do more, make more, BE MORE, but there is only so much time and energy that I can donate to my business right now, due to my two young daughters at home.

Exhilarating – when I do have a success, in the form of a sale, or when a gallery starts to carry my work, also when I am accepted into a prestigious exhibition

Energizing – gives my time in the studio a purpose. Having a deadline does the same thing.

Hop/Skip/Jump – This is my progress. I often feel that progress is made in small hops or skips, and if I'm lucky, a big jump.

Insomnia – sometimes my brain is so busy with ideas about the business or sculptures to make, or I'm so anxious about something, that it is hard for me to sleep.

Slow – Similar to Frustrating. The pace of making my pieces is so slow, and I get so frustrated. It often takes a week or two just to get a sculpture built. That's not including the glazing and firing either.

Future – I am excited about what the future holds. I think once I am able to find more balance, things will really start to fall in to place. Dreams – I am ready to live as large as I can. To go as big and as bright as I can!

Identity – Here in the USA, everyone seems to define you by your job. I guess I sort of do that to myself. On the weeks that I don't get in much work time in the studio, I feel like an imposter; that I am losing some of my identity, some of myself. But on those days that I make good progress in the studio, I feel invincible! It's so energizing!

Example – I definitely want to be a good example for my two girls. I want them to see me doing what I love and going after my creative dreams. I want to give them the courage to that in their lives.

Stephanie Amos:

Diverse – My business, KoiStudios, is not just a studio that sells and promotes paintings, but pottery, photography and sculpture too!

Global - KoiStudios sells art worldwide.

Intriguing - I am able to work in a broad spectrum of mediums. I would like to think this makes my business intriguing to others.

Creative - I have always been a creative person and I try to be creative throughout my business, from the work I create and sell to my website, blog, and networking.

Unique - I have always been told I am a unique individual and I'd like to think that carries through in my work and business.

Motivated - Making art is my passion and that is more than enough to be motivated to have a creative business!

Imaginative - You have to be and have a creative business!

Online - I've been selling art online for the past seven years. KoiStudios is definitely an online business.

Devoted - In order to have a successful creative business, you have to be devoted and believe in what you do. That, I am!

Dynamic - KoiStudios is always changing with new works of art, new ideas, and constant evolution

Leanne Wargowsky:

HAPPINESS - DREAMS - COLORFUL - INSPIRING - UPLIFTING - VIBRANT - SAFE - MOTIVATING - HONEST - KIND

Words. So powerful.

It is my wish that my words will bring **happiness** to those who read them. It is my wish that my art will always add a **colorful** and **vibrant** energy to those who see it. It is my wish to put out into the world all that is **safe**, that is **honest,** and that is **uplifting** and **kind**. It is my wish to **inspire** and **motivate** others by the things I say and do. It is my wish that my art and my words will remind people of the **dreams** within their own hearts. It is my wish that I can remind others to have faith in the spirit of those around them, and help them find the truest potential within themselves. My business has a long way to go to get to this, but I believe that by reminding myself of these words each and every day, I can reach it.

Jan Avellana:

Transition, Connection, Commencement, Sentimental, Draining, Soulful, Time Consuming, Disorganized, Becoming, Fruitful.

As you can see from my list of words, my business is in transition and is honestly a mix of blessings and hardship right now. Hazelnut Cottage is still all of the good things it once was—soulful, sentimental, a point of deep connection with others—but transitions as they are, can also be draining, a time of disorganization and confusion. Also, my custom hand stamped items are time consuming to make.

Still, even with all of the challenges I am going through right now in my business, I can see that this is a season of commencement, a time of new beginnings and a time of becoming more of who God created me to be.

Finally, I chose the word "fruitful" because even with the ups and downs, Hazelnut Cottage has been a source of fruitfulness financially (some seasons more than others) as well as creatively, allowing me to start with a manageable do-it-from-home product, to setting me off towards my mixed-media dreams!

YOUR TURN:

In rapid fire fashion, write down 10 words that describe your business. Share your thoughts on these words.

Question #7

WHAT WOULD YOU CONSIDER THE 'FAVORITE' MISTAKE IN YOUR BUSINESS?

They who dream by day are cognizant of many things which escape those who dream only by night.

Edgar Allan Poe

I have wanted badly to be featured on the etsy series "Quit your day job." Each and every interview features a crafty entrepreneur who is soaring to the top of his/her life creating something with paper or fiber or fabric or wood. I want to be that person who can charge the right amount of money to hit the sweet spot of not having to worry about if I am doing the right thing with my career.

Here's the problem: I love making things BUT the things I make have to be quick creations because my attention span is short. I am the magpie chasing after the next shiny thing. I have tried to sit down and create a large amount of my popular items but I find that I am miserable doing that.

One day I got an order for my affirmation bracelets. The person wanted 50 of them in two different colors with the word 'ballet' on them. "Oh it's a sign!" I thought. My word for this year is dance! Maybe this will lead to more referrals. More sales. Maybe after 3 years I have finally stumbled upon it. So when I created the first 5 to show her, she sent me an email with these words:

"Oh I did not realize they would be in block lettering. Can you try writing the word some other way?" And with that, I thought OK what's next.

I realize now I can thank this woman. I had moved out of my comfort zone to test my entrepreneurial spirit. The energy was just in the wrong place. No one's fault really. But it encouraged me to look for and to SEE what it is I really want to do to quit my day job.

JEAN SIMROSE:

Not advertising my business, not networking more and not putting myself 'out there'. Modesty is part of my Canadian culture and has subdued my confidence in my creativity and ability to be successful. My new plan is to: blog more often, advertise by starting a Facebook page for my business and networking more.

Alease McClenningham:

Not blogging so often. Since I have reduced the amount of blog post I submit weekly- I have seen a jump in my traffic. I know the reason why- it's because I am posting more quality and informative blog post- which is driving in a lot more traffic.

Kelly Warren:

Sheryl Crow's "My Favorite Mistake" just popped in my head. Wow, this is a tough question. I think I'll take a different twist on this. It's not the mistakes I've made that have been those "happy accidents" that pop in my head. It's the mistakes I've made for which I've come up with ingenious solutions that come to mind. These usually involve injury. It's rare that I get through an arts festival without an injury or two. I'm usually traveling by myself, so anyone who has done shows can tell you that setting up and breaking down your booth by yourself is a huge challenge (and many would say a mistake). I am very accident prone, so my favorite mistakes have been the wacky solutions I come up with to tend to my injuries, usually smashed, cut or pinched fingers earned when setting up or breaking down my tent, specifically. I've found that in lieu of a bandage, which I never seem to have on hand, a napkin stuffed in my glove box after my last trip to Burger King and a strip of duck tape make a great stand in.

Having that ingenuity transfers well to running a creative business. You have to learn to quickly think on your feet and determine how to quickly overcome setbacks. Mistakes become "favorite mistakes" when you view them through a different lens and really think about what you can learn from them. "Who needs band aids when you have napkins and duct tape?" can easily translate to "Who needs all those extra fancy supplies when I can create wonderful outcomes with what I have on hand?" Food for thought. We all have what we need. We just need to look at another way to use it.

Jan Avellana:

This is a hard question to answer...I think I'd say that going into jewelry was a mistake from the beginning in some ways. I know that answer might surprise some people. What I mean by this is that I can see now more of who I am, and that I really am not about jewelry and fashion and adornment, per se—not that these things are bad, just that they are not my passions. I was drawn to creating hand stamped jewelry because of the words, the sentiments that each piece holds. Do you see? Hazelnut Cottage was my first steps towards making my way back to my artistic roots. This baby step has given me courage to venture out onto new paths, it has given me a tribe of fellow artists to belong to, along with having been my schooling—I've learned so much about running a home-based business, including how to nurture an online presence—all of this through Hazelnut Cottage, my "favorite mistake."

Kelly Thiel:

I had trouble with this question. I don't have any great favorite mistakes, but I can say that I spent years doing small craft shows that didn't really interest me. I did these shows for one main reason – my mother. My mom was a potter, and she and I did these shows together. They weren't all great money-makers (in fact, I was lucky to break even on some of them!), but I did them so that I could spend time with my mother and have a fun experience together. Was it worth it? Oh, yes. Every single yucky little show we did was fun because we were together. Was it great for my business? Nope. But I did learn A LOT about the craft show business and booth displays.

Leanne Wargowsky:

I have to say that one of my 'favorite' mistakes was learning to listen to my creative heart and know that you can't force it. If you don't feel it . . . you shouldn't do it. Time and time again I found myself truly FORCING myself to produce. FORCING myself to create. I think most creative souls would agree that creativity often comes in spurts. Sometimes you have so many creative ideas that you feel them bursting from your seams. Other times, you might be empty . . . without a single thought in mind. It's ok. Forgiving yourself and allowing yourself these moments of 'rest' are so important. It is ok to leave it for a while, when you need to. Forcing the art might be a big mistake, and one that ends up taking more creative energy from you than you realize.

Nolwenn Petitbois:

I believe that there are no real mistakes, but that instead there are happy accidents. Happy because there is a lesson in every experiences we live (yes, even the hardest more painful ones).

I would say that my «favorite» mistake in my business is this desire to always learn more (by buying books, taking online classes, going to workshop). It's a mistake because I have already plenty of the answers I am usually looking for in those media and just don't trust myself enough about that, and that I spend money (too much) to learn, where I should spend it in more reasonable things like marketing and things geared toward moving forward in my ideas.

Stephanie Amos:

I would have to say my favorite mistake is when I learned the hard way about shipping artwork. When I made my first online sale, it was a triptych painting, each canvas being a 12×12, so it wasn't very big. I remember being so excited about the sale and not thinking too much about the cost of shipping. I took it to the nearest UPS shipping store which happened to be only a few blocks from my apartment. When it was all said and done, I ended up paying about half of what the painting was sold for! Each sale after the first was filled with trial and error and still to this day, it can sometimes be a guessing game. But now I am thankful for those favorite mistakes that lead us to the knowledge and wisdom we can share with others and use for our own purpose!

YOUR TURN:

WHAT WOULD YOU CONSIDER THE 'FAVORITE' MISTAKE IN YOUR BUSINESS?

QUESTION #8

The Balance question – *WHAT DOES IT MEAN TO YOU AND HOW IS IT WORKING FOR YOU?*

> *Never underestimate the power of dreams and the influence of the human spirit. We are all the same in this notion: The potential for greatness lives within each of us.*
>
> \- Wilma Rudolph

I am finally ready to admit it: I do not believe there is such a thing as balance. I think that there are times in your life that CERTAIN AREAS of your life are calling for focused attention. And by listening to that inner knowing about where your attention needs to be placed, you ultimately are tending to what you need to and you will have a sense of peace even if your to-dos are not being completed.

Case in point: as a military wife, I have had to stay very clear about how much energy I can put into my business. When my hubby is deployed I shift the time I work on my business to early morning or late nights. I feel like I would be doing a disservice to my little one to not have access to both parents because I am trying to reach a business goal. I have even put my business on vacation mode in the most stressful time. But now that she has gone to school, I can then prioritize my business to rise higher on the list

Then there are times where my creative juices are in overload and I KNOW I must make room for those new ideas. So I make dinners in advance or we do cold cuts for a few days because I have to tend to the muse.

Guilt I think is just a part of this thing called life. We would love to do it all and do it well. But I believe peace of mind calls for something different. And at the end of the day, this is what helps me to prioritize my life.

KELLY WARREN:

This is the picture I've been using as my "headshot" on the 101010 Project participants' blogs. I first shared it with you, and my thoughts behind it, here when I talked about the importance of not taking yourself too seriously. What led up to this picture speaks perfectly to my perspective on "The Balance Question: What does it mean to you and how is it working for you?"

I've enjoyed reading everyone else's response to this question, and it's further affirmed my belief that there is no such thing as balance. Our days ebb and flow based on what's currently most important. That desire to work on a new jewelry piece can quickly be pushed aside by a child with a scraped knee, the book that you wanted to work on can be pushed aside by a hug from a sweet little girl who wants to snuggle on the couch for a little while, and those photos you've been needing to edit can quickly be sidetracked by the latest dance routine presented to you right next to your desk. Add a full-time job, a very sick cat, and knee surgery to that mix and balance goes out the window.

So for me, some days things just "work." Other days they just don't, and that's okay. I've often heard people say that they haven't been able to work on their art because "life just gets in the way." I tend to look at the reverse of that. Those every day "life" moments are the most important parts of our journey. I think when we make the most of those precious moments; the art will come in its time and on its schedule. It's taken me a while to accept that, and I'm sure it's a far different type of life balancing act that those who work at their art full-time juggle, but realizing that those everyday moments are the most important piece of any given day has brought me a focus and a peace that was missing.

At the end of one of my all-time favorite movies, *FIELD OF DREAMS*, James Earl Jones as Terrance Mann says, "People will come, Ray. People will most definitely come." That's how I feel about my art and my time to do it and finding that mysterious, non-existent balance. "Time will come, Kelly. Time will most definitely come..." And when it does, I'll grab it. But for now, I'll take whatever little snippets I can take while enjoying what's number one on my list, my family, because Lord knows, the day will soon come when my girls will be teenagers and think they are far too cool to hang out with Mama.

NOLWENN PETITBOIS:

SO, NOLWENN, HOW DO YOU HANDLE BALANCE? For me, balance means I can dedicate equal attention and love to both my creative life and personal life. It means that none feels forgotten. And that I enjoy everything about it (being in my studio, playing with the kids, talking to my husband, cooking...). Balance means I am at peace with myself, with what I do and how I do it.

Jean Simrose:

Working at home is difficult for me because it means separating my home from my business. I have trouble avoiding distractions that seem to take priority over my work. I always vow to be more disciplined in my work and to give it my "all" without feeling that I should be doing something else. My plan is to decide what proportions work for me (50% work, 50% home?) and to make up a schedule to follow. My goals in both my home life and my business are to be more productive and get more projects completed.

Kelly Thiel:

"This is a HUGE issue for me. Balance, in my small world, means having quality time for my art and for my family. My family comes first, but a near second is my art. I have realized that I am BY FAR a happier person, thus a better mom, when I have creative time. This is a daily struggle for me. Some days I get it just right, and other days I don't. I am always, always, interested in how other artist parents juggle the day-to-day life with kids and art.

It's amazing to me what a good couple of hours in the studio can do for my mood. If I feel like I've gotten a decent amount of work done in the studio, then I can be so much happier in my role as Mom. My soul is happier and I have achieved Balance! Success!!"

Alease McClenningham:

It means saying No to activities that don't increase my bottom line. It has really worked out well to have a business coach. He makes me elevate every new activity as a money item on my balance sheet.

Sonya McCllough:

Recently I've decided for myself ... the only balance that truly works is that found in nature. So, I begin, again & again. Because trying to do it in any other way, has yet to work for me. But, what works better for me is to openly admit to Winter, whenever winter comes. If winter comes in the mist of the heat of summer ... than Winter it is.

Stephanie Amos:

The word **balance** means a great deal to me. It means finding that inner peace while actually living the life you were meant to live AND function in society as a good person. It also means that I have to make time to create every day in the midst of completing daily chores, caring for my family and being there for friends. There are days when it all falls into place and then there are other days when the word **BALANCE** hasn't even made its way into my vocabulary. But for the most part, I am a very balanced person (or so I would like you to think!)

Leanne Wargowsky:

Balance . . . Augh. Does that answer how it is working for me? In all seriousness, balance is a challenge for the people who want it all- a family, their own business, a soul filled life. And me? I'm one of those people. I worked for over 25 years in healthcare; the last eight of those years were spent as a mother, too. During my time as both a full-time employee and a mom, I felt like I was not meeting the needs of either roles (my job and my children).

Now that I am no longer in healthcare, I have had much more time to devote to my children during these early years when I feel they need it most. However, finding time for my new creative business is a challenge. Having a supportive partner in life is huge, and learning to accept help from others is another key (I gave up trying to be Wonder Woman long ago. I mean, I love the outfit, but it never looked quite right on me.) So, I say 'no' to things when I have to. I say 'yes' to help when I really need it. And I'm learning more and more the importance of having a schedule and sticking to it. Family time is family time. Business time is business time. And God willing, I'll continue to be right there in the middle of them both.

Jan Avellana:

"Next question please! Hah. I am so bad about being a balanced individual. For a long time, I have let my business consume most of my waking hours. I do not recommend this to anyone! However, the truth is, when you are building a business—especially when you have no business background and are learning everything for the first time—there is a huge learning curve. If you add to this the need to immediately produce an income as well as care for young children, it can be a very overwhelming venture.

Balance for me means that work is done during reasonably sane work hours and that it does not bleed over into all the other aspects of my life. Balance means being able to attend to my family and enjoy them, without feeling the need or guilt to work all the time. Balance means being able to practice self-care, spiritually, emotionally, mentally and physically."

YOUR TURN:

HOW DO YOU HANDLE BALANCE?

QUESTION #9

What do you need to STOP DOING in your business?

I choose to rise up out of that storm and see that in moments of desperation, fear, and helplessness, each of us can be a rainbow of hope, doing what we can to extend ourselves in kindness and grace to one another. And I know for sure that there is no them – there's only us.
-
Oprah Winfrey

I NEED TO STOP READING BOOKS ON HOW TO DO BUSINESS BETTER AND GET TO WORK. HAVE YOU EVER FOUND YOURSELF HERE? YOU FEEL LIKE YOU NEED TO READ ANOTHER ARTICLE ON SOCIAL MEDIA OR TAKE ONE MORE ONLINE BUSINESS COURSE OR GET MORE ADVICE?

I CAN BECOME OBSESSED WITH THE INFORMATION GATHERING. BUT HERE IS THE THING. I BET YOU (LIKE ME) KNOW ENOUGH TO, AS DANIELLE LAPORTE OF WHITE HOT TRUTH SAYS,

"LAUNCH AND LEARN."

WHEN I FINALLY TOOK THE LEAP TO GET CERTIFIED AS A LIFE COACH, GUESS WHEN THE INSTRUCTORS THOUGHT IT WAS 'SAFE' TO GIVE ME A GREEN LIGHT TO COACH: THE VERY FIRST WEEK. I THOUGHT, 'HOW IN THE WORLD CAN THEY THINK I AM READY?'

BUT YOU KNOW WHAT?

I WAS READY.

I AM READY.

Alease McClenningham:

TAKING ON CLIENTS WHO DON'T MATCH MY TARGET AUDIENCE AND WHO LACK THE BASIC SKILL SETS TO BE SUCCESSFUL IN AN ONLINE BUSINESS. IT SOUNDS MEAN- BUT I'VE REALIZED THAT IT HAS BECOME A WASTE OF MY TIME AND WE KNOW TIME IS MONEY.

Nolwenn Petitbois:

I NEED TO STOP COMPARING MYSELF WITH OTHER ARTISTS. WHETHER IT'S THEIR ART (AND THE «OOOOH I WISH I HAD CREATED THIS FIRST»), OR THEIR APPARENT SUCCESS.

I KNOW IT'S USELESS AND JUST MAKES ME FEEL SORRY FOR MYSELF (YAY FOR PITY PARTIES FROM TIME TO TIME, NOTHING BETTER TO START ON A NEW FOOT AFTERWARDS!).

Kelly Warren:

I LEARNED WHAT I NEEDED TO STOP DOING IN MY BUSINESS ABOUT TWO YEARS AGO. I THINK THE BIGGEST MISTAKE A CREATIVE BUSINESS OWNER CAN MAKE IS COMPARING HERSELF TO OTHER CREATIVES. BECAUSE NONE OF US IS EXACTLY ALIKE, WE ALL BRING SOMETHING A LITTLE DIFFERENT TO THE TABLE. AND WHAT WE EACH BRING TO THE TABLE IS SPECIAL IN ITS OWN WAY AND CAN'T BE COMPARED TO ANYONE ELSE.

I LOVE ALL THE STAMPINGTON PUBLICATIONS...SOMERSET STUDIO, ART JOURNALING, SEW SOMERSET, ETC, BUT FOR A WHILE THERE I HAVE TO ADMIT I STARTED SEEING THE SAME TYPES OF ART OVER AND OVER AGAIN. AND IT REALLY WASN'T THE TYPE OF ART I WAS ATTRACTED TO. WAS IT ART THAT WAS SELLING? MAYBE IT WAS, AS IT WAS CERTAINLY ART THAT WAS GETTING PUBLISHED. BUT WHAT I REALIZED WAS THAT I HAD TO STOP COMPARING MYSELF TO WHAT EVERYONE ELSE WAS DOING AND JUST DO WHAT MADE

ME HAPPY INSTEAD. IF A PARTICULAR STYLE OF JEWELRY WAS TAKING OFF, I LEARNED THAT IT WAS IMPORTANT TO ME TO NOT FOLLOW THAT TREND. I NEEDED TO STAY TRUE TO ME. OR IF I WAS SEEING A SIMILAR THEME IN SO MANY MIXED MEDIA PIECES, THAT DIDN'T MEAN THAT THAT WAS HOW I NEEDED TO STYLE MY WORK IF I REALLY DIDN'T CARE FOR THAT STYLE. SURE, LOOK TO OTHERS FOR INSPIRATION IF YOU FEEL YOU MUST—I CERTAINLY DO AT TIMES—BUT DON'T COMPARE YOURSELF TO OTHERS. BE TRUE TO YOU.

Sonya McCllough:

I NEED TO STOP DOING THE EASY. PLAIN AND SIMPLE. SOME TALENTS COME EASY TO US. BECAUSE THOSE TALENTS HAVE ALREADY BEEN HONED, HONORED AND ACHIEVED. I NEED TO STOP DOING THE EASY. YOU WHO ARE READING THIS ... NEED TO STOP DOING THE EASY. WE NEED TO STOP DOING THE EASY AND DO THE HARD.

DELIVERANCE IS FOUND IN THE HARD PLACES. WHERE ARE YOUR HARD PLACES?

Kelly Thiel:

I NEED TO FIND A WAY TO STOP SPENDING SO MUCH TIME ON THE SMALLER ITEMS I MAKE FOR WHOLESALING. THESE ITEMS HELP TO BRING IN MONEY, BUT THEY EAT UP ALL OF MY STUDIO TIME, SO THAT I CAN NEVER MOVE ON TO BIGGER PROJECTS. THERE ARE SO, SO MANY THINGS I WANT TO CREATE IN THE STUDIO, AND ONLY A FRACTION OF THEM WILL EVER GET MADE AT THIS RATE! IN SOME WAYS, I LIKE MAKING THESE SMALLER THINGS, BECAUSE I CAN WORK OUT IDEAS OR COLORS ON SMALLER PIECES BEFORE MOVING ON TO A BIGGER PIECE. BUT WHAT ENDS UP HAPPENING, IS THAT I SUDDENLY NEED 30 SMALL PIECES FOR A SHOW OR AN ORDER, AND THEN ALL MY TIME IS SUDDENLY SUCKED UP MAKING SMALL PIECES AND NONE OF THE OTHER SCULPTURES IN MY HEAD

EVER GET STARTED.

MY HUSBAND HAS PUSHED ME FOR YEARS TO GET AN ASSISTANT TO HELP WITH THESE THINGS. AND I THINK I WILL EVENTUALLY DO IT. I'M EXCITED BY HAVING HELP IN THE STUDIO; GETTING THEM TO HELP WITH SOME OF THE SMALL TASKS INVOLVED IN MAKING THE PIECES, SO THAT WE CAN MAKE MORE OF THEM FASTER. SOMETIMES I WORK BETTER TOO, WHEN SOMEONE IS THERE WITH ME, CREATING.

I THINK THAT ONCE I HAVE SOME FORWARD MOMENTUM, AND THINGS ARE GETTING BUSY AGAIN, I WILL START LOOKING FOR AN ASSISTANT. IT WILL BE HARD – I KNOW I'LL HAVE TO FIND THE RIGHT PERSON TO SHARE MY STUDIO WITH – BUT IN THE END, I THINK THAT IT WILL BE RIGHT FOR THE BUSINESS.

Leanne Wargowsky:

QUESTIONING AND INTERNALIZING EVERYTHING . . . AND THEN . . . STALLING. I TRULY, LIKE SO MANY OTHERS, AM MY OWN WORST ENEMY. I NEED TO STOP LISTENING TO THE VOICES THAT TELL ME "I CAN'T" AND ONLY FOCUS ON THOSE THAT TELL ME "I CAN!" I NEED TO BELIEVE IN MY GOALS, IN MY ABILITIES, AND MOVE FORWARD. A DEAR FRIEND OF MINE ALWAYS SAYS, "IF YOU AREN'T GOING TO HELP ME, THEN GET OUT OF MY WAY SO I CAN GET THE JOB DONE!" , AND SHE TRULY EXEMPLIFIES THAT IN ALL THAT SHE DOES. WHEN I LOOK AT THE PAST, I FIND I HAVE WASTED A GREAT DEAL OF TIME IN THE "WHAT IF . . . " STAGE. MY GOAL FOR THIS NEXT YEAR? TO STOP LOOKING IN THE PAST, AND FOCUS ON MOVING FORWARD TO THE *BRIGHT YELLOW* FUTURE.

Stephanie Amos:

PROCRASTINATING! I SEE MANY PEOPLE WITH CREATIVE BUSINESSES THAT ARE SO INVOLVED WITH THEIR ART COMMUNITY, CREATING NON-STOP, AND NETWORKING ALL AT

THE SAME TIME. I FIND MYSELF STANDING ON THE SIDELINES WONDERING WHY I'M NOT DOING THE SAME THING. I HAVE NARROWED IT DOWN TO PROCRASTINATION. I UNDERSTAND THAT IT HAPPENS TO THE BEST OF US, BUT I HAVE A SEVERE CASE OF THE DISEASE THAT TENDS TO LINGER INSTEAD OF DISAPPEARING. STAYING FOCUSED ON YOUR GOALS AND CREATING ANY CHANCE YOU GET WILL BE MY FUTURE AMMUNITION TO PREVAIL!

YOUR TURN:

What do you need to STOP DOING in your business?

Question #10:
Who is your business muse?

I burned in the unutterable beauty of being alive.

-

John Peale Bishop

For me, this person is **Danielle LaPorte**

Grounded. Savvy. Authentic. Sincere.

She encourages me to do a little more of what I want to do in business and a little less of what I don't want to do every day.

She challenges me to launch my products and services and learn from it.

She asks me what I need to stop doing this week.

She sends a burning question to my inbox every week that helps me stay authentic to what I want to be in life.

She scoffs at the idea that there is such a thing as life balance.

She trusts her instincts.

Yeah, she helps me to be a little more myself and what I want to stand for in life and in business.

Sonya McCllough:

My current female business muse is Sarah Mae. Yes, I too have a CRUSH.

Kelly Thiel:

I haven't found one person that fits all the requirements. I've started to look more closely at a handful of predominantly clay artists whose careers I'd sort of like to follow. The other side of it is professional photographers. My husband, who is a pro photographer, introduces me to other blogs and business ideas that are popular in the photography world. They seem to have a lot of ideas and thoughts that I find to be more exciting and forward-thinking. I'm still working on this, and I am excited by the thought of finding the one person to be my MUSE.

Nolwenn Petitbois:

It's not an easy question. I don't think I have somebody specific in mind. But any woman who had figured out how to have a thriving creative business while managing a social life, a family life and a personal life in general is my Muse.

Jan Avellana:

I'd have to say that Kelly Rae Roberts is my business muse. The woman has reached a level of financial success and artistic stride that I can only dream about reaching one day. Oh how I aspire!

This being said, there are so many other artists who are perhaps lesser known that are making a very happy and meaningful living for themselves and their families, each having found their OWN path. I am inspired by each and every artist out there who has found a way to incorporate their loves and passions into their lives, whether or not they make art for a "living".

Leanne Wargowsky:

Like many dreamers and "flyers" from Kelly Rae Roberts "Flying Lessons" e-course, I would be amiss to not mention Kelly Rae Roberts as my business muse. For years I have followed her presence online and watched as she was lead by her inner voice to a world of success. She continues to expand her business by leaps and bounds, and I am in awe the work, dedication, and success she has had.

In addition, I find myself a great admirer of the business of Teahouse Studio and Mati Rose (and partners). Teahouse Studio is a dream to me, I only wish I lived closer so I could move in! Mati's art is so whimsical and bright, it makes me smile each time I see it. I love what she has done. And Donna Downey . . . creative and business genius. There are so many more out there that have done it, and each time I stumble upon a new business and artist who inspires me, I soak up all the positive energy I can and tell myself, "You can do this, too! Just . . . DO IT!" My wish for us all . . . that we ALL do it!

Alease McClenningham:

The ladies in the 101010 project (aka the Spark and Inspire collaboration). They have been an inspiration to me and I love learning new things from them.

Stephanie Amos:

My business muse just so happens to be Robin Norgren, the creator of this project! I have been in awe of this amazing woman since I met her online a couple years ago through the e-course, Flying Lessons. She not only is a mother, a military wife and a business owner, but a faithful follower of God who shares her love of life and her faith with everyone she meets. Robin is honest about who she is and what she wants out of her business. Just this year, I met Robin in person for the first time. I felt as if I've known her my entire life! Robin inspires me to make business goals, learn and connect with others like us, and no matter what...move forward and never give up!

Kelly Warren:

Maybe this is a little old-fashioned and corny, but my muses are my children. Though I've been a creative person since I was a child myself, it was the birth of my twin girls that really pushed me to move forward to creating a formalized business.

When my girls were born, I wanted one of those mother's bracelets that included your children's names. I looked online and saw several styles, none of which were less than $100. At that point I said, "I can do this." While I'd dabbled in all sorts of arts and crafts up to that point, I had never made jewelry, so I headed down to my local bead shop, showed the wonderful ladies there what I wanted to do, and got started. That was just the beginning. As I was growing my jewelry designs skills, I discovered the wonderful world of artists' blogs, which led to me mixed media and reignited my love of photography.

So here I am today, all mixed up creating in a variety of media and loving every minute of it. And even as my girls were that little muse of a kick start to get me moving, they are still what keep me going. I love to create with them. I love to create for them. I love to see the little sparks in their eyes as they bring their creations to life. And all this comes together with our annual Mermaids and Mamas Artful Adventure, this year in its third year. My girls and I gather together with other mamas and daughters and spend a weekend in a fun little camp making art. It's a wonderful thing! You can read more about it here: http://purplecottageretreats.blogspot.com

YOUR TURN:

Who is your business muse?

Question #11

Is it necessary for your business to line up with your soul purpose? What value is there to having that aligned?

I don't want to hurry it. That itself is a poisonous twentieth-century attitude. When you want to hurry something, that means you no longer care about it and want to get on to other things.

Robert M. Pirsig, Zen and the Art of Motorcycle Maintenance

I have always thought that everyone had the same answer to this question: yes OF COURSE you would want to have your business line up with your soul purpose. Then I had a client the other day explain why she did not think this was necessary. Her words: "well my family is my soul purpose... everything else is just about making money."

It made me sit back and think about whether or not my thoughts would change now that I heard another perspective. And guess what? It has! I have been chugging along for about 4 years now attempting to integrate my career with my soul purpose. But what I realize is really my soul purpose DEEP DOWN is very close to this women's assessment. I want to make sure that my family ALWAYS feels like I am there for them no matter what. And this has been tested quite a bit with my husband being deployed with the military the majority of the past three years and my choice to stay home with my daughter to make that transition easier on her.

I have tried very hard to keep that dream alive of integrating the two. At this point I do a ton of late night and early morning work in order to keep that dream at least burning a little on the back burner. And I dare say that in the future it would seem a reasonable expectation to go for it with my hubby retiring from the military in five years and my girl getting older. But for now I am satisfied with just doing all I know to do to run my business but keeping my soul purpose clear: to make the best life possible for my kids.

Paula Joerling:

I guess for me, it is. I have had odd jobs here and there and it never feels right. All I could think about was what I would be doing if I were back in the studio. I sometimes wish that I could be the type of person who could work a 9-5 job. Creating things gives me great satisfaction and is a part of my make up that I can't shake; nor do I want to. The value in having it aligned is being able to be what and who I am 24/7.

Shari Sherman:

YES! When you first start out, the primary focus is making money. After all, that's what a business is, right? And there is definitely a JOY in having someone pay you for something that you created. Wow! You feel like a "real artist", and you can easily start to believe that is where your value lies.

But I've learned that in order for your business to grow from a solid foundation, it must be based on an outpouring of your soul. That is where the true JOY multiplies! That is what will keep you going, keep you creating, keep you trying, and keeps the inspiration flowing. Otherwise, you will dry up from stress, you won't have time to let new ideas in, you will start to feel like you are on a production line, and the money will not be enough to keep you going. The value in realizing that what you are creating is important, is soul-connected, rather than just a vehicle to get what you need...Priceless!

Valerie Weller:

For me, there could be no other way. I am of the belief that creatives flow from their center- their core- their art spirit. The soul of an artist is fertile ground, where creative seeds are sown and art grows. When your business is in line with what your soul is about, it becomes an incredible gift to the world. Your work has deep connectivity. It speaks on many levels to others and allows for your heart to thrive.

The creative culture in business these days seems to be multi-faceted, with a more giving relationship toward its consumer. We are seeing more and more businesses allowing the space to give to causes and community, while still gaining abundance from their creative offerings to the world. I believe there is no doubt, working with my soul purpose in alignment with my business goals, will produce a deeper, richer and more joyful place in my life, my art and in what I put out into the world.

Stephanie Guimond:

I don't think it's necessary, no.

Some people are content and quite happy to exchange fair work for fair payment, where payment may be money, time, flexibility or anything else that allows them to fulfill their soul's purpose elsewhere. For example, someone may choose to become an independent consultant because it allows them a flexible schedule for travel; travel is their soul purpose, not the work.

Others look for more. For these folks, having business and soul align can be a powerful motivator and get them through the difficulties that come with starting a business and keeping it running.

I see value in both; it really depends on the individual. I suspect I fall somewhere in between.

Phyllis Dobbs:

Yes, it is very important to me to be true to myself and my style. In fact, if I don't feel something, it is hard for me to deviate. My business is based on how I feel and how I create. Otherwise, it would just be "work" and for me, my business is much more than that and is filled with passion about what I do.

Dani Keith:

I definitely think that discovering what feeds my soul and applying that discovery to my daily work has been essential to the success of my business.

Before starting and devoting my full time efforts to {dk} designs, I worked a traditional and corporate job; it was lucrative but soul crushing. The clarity that you get when you listen to that little voice inside out weighs the fear of starting something new, something creative, something that is all yours. Producing work that you believe in and that you have a passion for nourishes your soul and for me is one of my highest priorities.

YOUR TURN:

Is it necessary for your business to line up with your soul purpose? What value is there to having that aligned?

Question #12

Do you have a business mentor? What values does that offer to your experiences as a business owner?

> *Wherever you are is always the right place. There is never a need to fix anything, to hitch up the bootstraps of the soul and start at some higher place. Start right where you are.*
>
> *Julia Cameron*

This is one of the things I am going to put in place in 2012. I do not have an up close and personal mentor but I know that my business needs one. Over the last few years I have been relying on business books and e-courses – all good stuff and extremely valuable information was shared.

The problem is I think there comes a point in time where you hit a crossroad. You need to connect with someone face to face to help you craft goals that you are terrified of and yet someone is looking you dead in the eye and says 'you got this- go for it!"

I think we all need that. I know many of the traits of the entrepreneur have to do with drive and tenacity and willingness to go with that inner knowing. But when that is not the issue anymore but it is more of a 'what's next' that you are looking at... well I believe that is when you cannot continue on as a lone wolf.

Stephanie Guimond:

 I don't have a business mentor in the traditional sense where two people have a formal mentor/mentee relationship. I have identified individuals I admire for either their creative or business endeavors or both, who serve as role models and show me what's possible. I call them my *possibility tracks*. I guess you could say it's mentorship via observation and study.

In addition to my possibility tracks I converse with other businesswomen regularly either online or in person to exchange goals, ideas, challenges and support. I am tremendously grateful for these circles of kindred spirits. I guess you could say it's mentorship via group sharing.

I think I would enjoy the connection that comes by apprenticing with someone who's been through many of the joys and challenges I'm currently navigating, but in the absence of that relationship, there is no lack of ways to learn and be inspired. Learning and inspiration are always of value no matter what form they take.

Phyllis Dobbs:

No, but I have received a lot of help over the years. When I started, I talked to designers/artists doing the same thing. I am also a member in several forums where we act as sounding boards to each other. Everything I learn is of great value to my business - whether it's taking steps forward or avoiding pitfalls.

Valerie Weller:

There are quite a few people that I look to as mentors in business. It's hard to think of only one, when you are influenced by so many. Two that come to mind immediately, are Kelly Rae Roberts & Brian Schnetzer of Aunt Sadies Candles. I admire how both structure their business, work through their soul purpose, and how they connect with the community that brings them their success.

I've come to know Kelly Rae through her original art and Flying Lessons e-course that I took two years ago. And I must say that her e-courses have been part of the core foundation in redirecting my business. I learned so much from her, not only from her teachings, but also from watching her business grow tremendously in the past few years. Just by taking a peek at her website www.kellyraeroberts.com would confirm a savvy, down to earth artist and business woman.

My dear friend Brian runs a candle company that started out in Boston, and now is headquartered in Vermont. He started Aunt Sadie's Candles back in the mid nineties. His business grew and flourished with a brick and mortar shop, online product and wholesale accounts in high end stores such as Anthropologie, to smaller boutiques like Kitson in Los Angeles. Being a close friend for many years, I watched his business grow and prosper. Created from his soul, to honor the life of his dear grandmother "Aunt Sadie", I've been able to learn much about company culture, as well as starting up and keeping a business through the years. It's great to have a few mentors' willing to share with you, allowing you to learn more about developing your own path. Being a creative in "business" can sometime seems like opposites- I'd rather create than sell, market, or ship goods... but having mentors to share with, brings encouragement, and reassurance in business.

Paula Joerling:

Funny you should ask……..as of a few weeks ago, yes. I felt like I was hitting a wall and needed a shot in the arm. I do my best work when I am directed and I hadn't been getting much of that lately. I found a mentor through a friend and it's been really great having someone help me with some of the things I have been struggling with in my business.

It's always good to see your business through the eyes of someone who has been there and done that.

Dani Keith:

My mentor is amazing on two levels, she is an amazing metalsmith/creative entrepreneur and I am lucky to have studied with her, plus she is a very successful gallery owner {one of my future goals} While there are numerous gifts that we give and receive when working in a collaborative studio space, what I learn from her is both how she continually feeds her creative muse and how that talent and creativity translates into her business model.

She is an amazing example of generous talent and savvy businesswoman. Observing a person who has achieved my definition of success has had a dramatic effect on how my business model has evolved and been honed.

Shari Sherman:

I don't have a traditional business mentor, but I can see the tremendous value in having someone guide you...to help you avoid some speed bumps, as well as recognize opportunities that you might not see. Maybe that will manifest for me in the future as I begin to explore the world of art licensing. What I do have is an amazing group of creative women that I belong to called the VoGs. They offer me support, guidance, and encouragement to keep pursing my creative dream.

Laura Otero:

I have had a wonderful mentor in a broad business sense that has looked out for me and encouraged me since 2006. Like a grandfather, he was a former boss who has kept in touch. He gave me the courage to walk away from the news industry, where I was a digital sales director. He has always seen my worth, and has encouraged me to continue to grow regardless of where I may be employed.

That said, he isn't an expert in the online marketing/design world. When I began designing websites and managing social media, I found it challenging to find a mentor willing to share successes and challenges with me, and (especially) a pricing structure. Several years later, I have learned that I'm the only one who can put a price on my time. I've gone from a professional who was undercharging for my work to a person who knows my value and can put a fair price on my services.

If you are starting out in the design biz or consulting world, I would recommend providing an estimate of the time involved in your services, but always leaving room/protecting yourself with the freedom to charge hourly should the quote exceed the hours estimated for your work. This may be the biggest lesson I've learned in the past few years.

Looking for bold, brave souls living their dreams? Check out Kelly Rae Roberts, Beth Nicholls, Liv Lane and Andrea Schroeder. I've taken an e-course from Kelly and multiple e-courses from Andrea. I follow each of their blogs closely and celebrate in their successes. Watching each of them "dream big" and work hard for what they envision for their lives has been beyond inspiring.

YOUR TURN:

Do you have a business mentor? What value does that offer to your experiences as a business owner?

Question #13

What animal would represent your first year of business?

Love recognizes no barriers. It jumps hurdles, leaps fences, penetrates walls to arrive at its destination, full of hope.
-
Maya Angelou

I am smiling as I write this because I was going back and forth between a turtle and a finicky cat that hides under the bed and is easily spooked! I think I will go with the kitty cat. I did not tell anyone that I started my business on etsy. I was still contending with a serious identity crisis when I first started up in 2009. I was nursing some wounds on some dreams that had died about my life as a chaplain in the U.S. Navy.

I worked toward that goal for almost three years and after two rejections, I just felt aimless. Then low and behold when my husband was deployed with the military leaving me home alone with my two year old daughter... well aimless and lost definitely described me.

So funny how now I look back and realize that allowing that dream to just be what it was – unrealized and tragic – and move into the what is next... well I can tell you this girl is NO LONGER the skittish kitty cat! More than anything it taught me that it is OK AND NOT ONLY OK BUT POSSIBLE to get a new dream...

Shari Sherman:

Even though my business began with dog paintings, I think I was more of a monkey! Like a crazy monkey...I was just so happy and excited to be out there, being an artist that I tried to do everything I could get into. Anything I hadn't tried before, I wanted to do it, just to do it. I was all over the place, which wasn't necessarily a bad thing. In fact, the experiences were invaluable. But from a business standpoint, that is not necessarily the most efficient, successful way. Now I try to operate more like a turtle...slow and steacy, deliberately taking steps, instead of jumping from here to there to waaay over there, like a crazy monkey!

PHYLLIS DOBBS:

I had to chuckle at this question. I started my business as Lucky Duck Designs and illustrated a lot of ducks for countless cross stitched items. So my answer is a duck. I was also given a lot of nicknames such as "Ducky" and "Ms. Duck".

I am in a huge network of people with the same type of business as mine. So I would go in a different direction. Tony Ford is the one I would love to sit and talk with. I have attended several of Tony's seminars and came away with so much information. In today's world, social media is so important for business so I would discuss the rapidly changing world of social media and technology and how to use it effectively with my business. (Tony Ford is the COO of ArtFire.com and the Technology Expert for the Craft and Hobby Association, CHA).

Valerie Weller:

Why a bird of course! I laugh, as I say this, because I tend to paint birds into my art frequently, and I am drawn to them in nature. We have many birdhouses in our yard, plants to attract them, and feeders to provide for them. I see them as spiritual little beings, organic in nature, with wings that they trust, to take them along paths, that only they know.

A brief little story- we had a small birdhouse, on a post in our yard for many years. The house was decorative with a very small hole- too small for any bird to nest in, so I thought. The summer before my daughter left for college, a little bird took up residence. I watched from my kitchen window as the poppa bird brought twigs, grasses and clippings to weave a place for momma to have the kiddos. I watched in amazement. This incredible process came at a most meaningful time of transition in my life. Could it be that this nest was intentionally put there for me to experience?

Three little eggs hatched at the end of summer. I watched three little birds fly off literally, a couple of days before my oldest daughter went away to college. I hold this sweet experience close to my heart; serving as a symbol of the "transitions" we all go through in life- my art process and business, being the current one. Those little birds embodied being brave, knowing when to fly, and trusting the spirit to guide them along the path put forth. Little birds... such meaningful little connectors in my art life.

Stephanie Guimond:

Turtle. Definitely the turtle because even though at some times the journey seems full & chaotic, overall I feel like it's been slow & steady - one action at a time. Sometimes I wish I worked faster, I'm experimenting with pace to see what works best. In the meantime I practice trust that even at my turtle pace I will reach a finish line someday soon so I can move to the next leg of the race.

Dani Keith:

an ant...those poor little buggers never stop, and neither did I!

I gave new meaning to chief, cook and bottle washer and I can say that the most identifying feeling I had was exhaustion. After my first year of business I took a really hard look at my practice and my return on investment...what I discovered is that I most definitely worked a lot harder than smarter and that needed to change. The good news is there are a lot of basics that need to be done that first year, but once they are done, they are DONE. I have been able to refine my production and fabrication times, and most importantly I have learned how to say 'no' I don't take every project that I am offered, I set time and space boundaries and most importantly in year two I remembered how to breathe...because breathing is GOOD!

Paula Joerling:

It's hard to remember back that far. It would have to be something that wants to go in a million different directions at once.

Laura Otero:

This is a tough one! I officially created my LLC in April of 2011 but have been doing freelance design/web work since as early as 2007. During my first few years in business, so much self-growth happened. I guess you could say I was an "eager beaver" at first.

I sometimes (unknowingly) undervalued my work and did not charge others fully for the time spent on various projects. I would accept projects big and small, leaving little time for family and self-care. I had some wonderful clients but also had a challenging experience where I learned the value of creating a business contract before beginning work.

Today, I'm more selective about who I do business with, more careful about the contract side of the work, and more protective of my time. If this sounds a little cautious, it's because I am more cautious. But on the flipside, I also truly enjoy who I work with and have more balance in my life. I'm hoping my business will continue to grow and flourish, more closely resembling a butterfly or maybe even a dolphin.

Expressive, flowing, with beauty and balance in the everyday happenings of my work.

I have always loved Kelly Rae Robert's art girlies, and especially love when they have butterfly wings (like this one). I'm drawn to the water and love living in Charleston, which is where dolphins come in. One of my recent paintings was a mermaid (seen on my Twitter background here or here for those reading via mobile) - another way I express my love of the water and the peace and clarity that it brings.

YOUR TURN:

What animal would represent your first year of business?

Question #14

What business/businesses have you chosen to model your business after?

Yes, I am a dreamer. For a dreamer is one who can find his way by moonlight, and see the dawn before the rest of the world.

Oscar Wilde

Curly Girl Designs is the music of my artistic life.

Seth Godin plays to my practical side of dreaming big.

Leigh of Curly Girl Designs had the drive and the talent to move into the competitive greeting card industry. I have been aware of her since about 2007 when I received one of Curly Girl Designs' friendship cards from a friend. The art on the front was like nothing I had ever seen before. Now I have come to realize the genre Leigh's work is in is called mixed media, a world I didn't realize was 'out there' until about 2010. Leigh exemplifies to me the girl with a dream and the stamina to see it through.

Seth Godin puts high marks on the use of creativity as the only means to get us out of our country's current recession. Godin reminds me that each one of us has the potential to be idea generators. We just need to be willing to stop pandering after the easy and THINK MORE creatively.

Dani Keith:

I am lucky to be represented by a gallery that really supports and celebrates the talent of the creatives that line the shelves and cases. Started by a maker of art jewelry that has been fabricating for over 20 years, LEDE Gallery & Studio has been an excellent business model to emulate. Combining the retail, commission and educational disciplines, most definitely helps me to hone my craft and clarify my business goals

Laura Otero:

I have been so inspired by Kelly Rae Roberts and Andrea Schroeder. Andrea's approach to business seems to fit so well into the processes I also employ when I know it's time to grow and change – art journaling, dreaming big, writing/blogging and working hard for it.

Kelly and Andrea have both struggled (and sometimes still do struggle) with the "self-doubt monsters." We all have them, and if we feed them, they grow.

I love that Kelly takes time to find her deepest, biggest dreams and work very hard to reach them.

My business approach for 2012 seems overly simplistic on paper – to work with 4 clients who I enjoy and who love and appreciate my work. This has been intentional – to leave time for family and artful adventures. As I make my way through the year, I may develop a more robust business plan.

Since leaving my traditional marketing job to gain more time for family, art and adventures, I'm focusing on treating each day as the gift that it is. As I enjoy my morning walk and coffee, I journal about my dreams and goals, and the steps needed to get there.

Phyllis Dobbs:

None specifically. But in networking over the years with people having the same type of business, I've morphed my business into what fits with what I want to accomplish. I've also learned a lot through seminars and conferences.

Shari Sherman:

It wasn't until recently that I had given this much deliberate thought. I think we can go along just trying to carve out our own paths, not really realizing that it is OK to cut through sections that someone else has cleared for us.

There are many businesses that I admire...Kelly Rae's being one of them. I just love seeing her process from beginning to NOW! Flying Lessons is an amazing business guide to help along the way. I would also say that I am choosing to model my business after Leonie Dawson (formerly Leonie Allan). Her Business Goddess e-course has been such a tremendous help in getting perspective on project development and business opportunity. I have the creativity, as we all do, but getting that to the point where it will generate income and growth is where these lovely models can really help. Mostly, they are models that say, "It CAN be done, and YOU CAN DO IT Too!"

Valerie Weller:

As there are a few mentors, there are a few businesses that inspire me with their creative business ideals. I have to say, the first art business that got me looking closely at creative business models was Kelly Rae Roberts.com. After taking her Flying Lessons e-course, and most recently Hello Soul Hello Business, I became acutely aware of the ever changing entrepreneurial field of art businesses. I started to see the many levels a business could be built upon, and how rewarding it can be to build a team that gives back.

The Zappo's company has a corporate culture that I respect and would love to model my business after. There are more and more businesses reflecting the "take care of your people" mentality- that employ people with "soul mission's that aligns with yours" and have a "give back to the community or world" connection.

Another one..."I Have a Bean Coffee Company" has a mission that I wholeheartedly admire. Their focus is on their product being in complete alignment with a "mission of community service".

And of course, my all time favorite... Kelly Rae Roberts, a creative entrepreneur that built her art business with all roads converging back to her art, heart, and what she gives out into the world.

When I look at these three companies, I see a lot of qualities that I'd like my own business to reflect as it grows bigger. To have a "soul" purpose guiding from the center, allows me to believe that I can achieve wonderful things.

Stephanie Guimond:

Truth be told I'm still figuring that out. Different businesses or solopreneurs influence different parts of what I currently offer or want to offer in the future. Here are a few people who are currently influencing my thoughts, actions and where I'd like to go:

- Barbara Winter at Joyfully Jobless for her multiple income streams under the umbrella of information packaging (in-person workshops, book, newsletter)
- Lisa Occhipinti and Kelly Rae Roberts for possible income streams related to my artwork (online sales, licensing, book, e-courses, in-person workshops, home art parties)
- Tara Gentile and Christine Kane for their approaches to coaching and consultation services/products (individual, group, information products - free and $, high-level programs)
- Leonie Dawson for how she consistently branded & produced her information products and the financial model of her membership circle

There are many good models out there from which I hope to glean wisdom with which I will weave a tailored one that works for me. I am grateful.

Paula Joerling:

To tell you the truth I have just been finding my own way. When I need help or direction I reach out to friends who do what I do. I have a licensing agent so I rely on them to do a lot of the business part.

YOUR TURN:

What business/businesses have you chosen to model your business after?

Question #15

At this moment, what one idea do you need to start executing for your business?

> "I hope you will go out and let stories happen to you, and that you will work them, water them with your blood and tears and your laughter till they bloom, till you yourself burst into bloom."
>
> Clarissa Pinkola Estés

The first thought that popped into my head is a quote by Nelson Mandela:

> "YOUR PLAYING SMALL DOES NOT SERVE THE WORLD. THERE IS NOTHING ENLIGHTENED ABOUT SHRINKING SO THAT OTHER PEOPLE WON'T FEEL INSECURE AROUND YOU. WE WERE BORN TO MANIFEST THE GLORY OF GOD WITHIN US. IT IS NOT JUST IN SOME; IT IS IN EVERYONE."

I admit it: I play small. I am unsure of what I am doing at times because there is no established road on how I will add value to the world. And I live in a circle where fear runs rampant in otherwise incredibly intelligent and talented people. So when I strike out on a new idea, I am met with mostly silence which you would think would be easy to push past but in fact is actually more taxing on the psyche. Silence offers nothing: approval or disapproval. Unless of course you KNOW that silence from certain people means DISAPPROVAL.

This is the year that I will build a tribe of like minded people in close proximity who can witness me and cheer me on. I don't need many; just 2 or 3. In that environment where my tribe is also struggling to push past fear and move into the harder things — the more value filled and world impacting things — there will be a safety to hear the NO when it needs to be said. At the same time the cheers will be heartfelt and genuine as each one watches the other change, grow, fail, redirect and ultimately succeed in ways that go far beyond running a successful business: a fulfilled and valuable part of society.

Dani Keith:

Collaboration...I have reached a certain rhythm in my production and I have achieved my expansion goals, what I need to do now is curate and collaborate with my fellow creatives. I believe that when you can bring talent and vision together it fuels your personal creativity. There is a power and energy that is created when people collaborate and the network and benefits of that effort are felt long after the event itself.

Paula Joerling:

I have decided to offer my own line of cards and paper goods and, hopefully show at the 2013 Stationery Show. So I need to shift productivity into high gear.

Phyllis Dobbs:

I would like to incorporate more teaching of classes as well as developing classes.

Shari Sherman:

Right NOW, the one idea that I need to start implementing is the idea that I CAN embrace and master the art of TIME MANAGEMENT. For the longest time, this has been a sticking point for me. So much so that it really had become incorporated into my STORY. I can't tell you how many times I would be up late the night before a show, printing, packing, making tags, and doing whatever other little jobs that could have been done earlier. Or how many projects I missed out on because I let the deadline loom nearer and nearer...all the while telling myself I work much better under pressure. Ha!

I am ready to turn the page and write a new chapter about planning ahead and keeping track of what I really want to be INVOLVED in (not just skimming by). It really is about making the commitment to AWARENESS about my business. (Tip: I have a little timer set RIGHT NOW, to help me stay on track while writing this...I really, really DO!)

STEPHANIE GUIMOND:

I am going to cheat and mention two ideas, but they're very closely related, I promise!

IDEA #1
I've already started executing this idea, it's a matter of moving it forward. I've recently worked with (very brave!) beta clients offering *GET CLEAR, GET MOVING* planning & goal setting consultation packages. There are several formats available to me in sharing this content and these offerings, each one with its relative pricing and potential income. A key next step in my business is to figure out which format to launch first and do it.

IDEA #2
I want to publish a foundational information product that would become an entry way into my brand and business (consultation services in this case, not art). The intention of this product is to offer a solution to a problem while "teaching" potential clients about my core philosophy and what they need to know before going further with me. I gleaned the concept from Tara Gentile. Her foundational product is The Art of Earning which deals with her money philosophy (that making money should be beautiful) and helps new readers work through money issues before working further with her,

therefore attracting people into more advanced programs who are already aligned with her views.

Laura Otero:

So difficult to choose just one idea! It's a tie between my need to start charging what I'm worth and my desire to create more personal/artful time for myself to recharge.

Making time for artful adventures every day is something I've started the summer out with more intentionally...whether that means taking a walk through the garden, snapping instagram photos for inspiration, playing in my art journal, or putting a brush to canvas.

I had dreams of an art studio space and they recently came to life, so I have more room to spread out my supplies and have fun. I've been painting on bigger canvases with new techniques. Time over at Kelly's studio playing in paint and mixed media have also been a part of my summer so far. Kelly and I met through Flying Lessons, and having an artsy friend in the area has been such a blessing.

Charging what I'm worth can be a tough one, but being more selective about the projects I take on and quoting a more realistic number in terms of time investment has helped me to make great progress in this area as well. When I feel tempted to undercharge, I think about my family and the fact that I am shortchanging all of us, not just myself.

Funny thing is, the more time I take for myself in terms of art and journaling; the more confident I am in business. Knowing one's worth is always the first step!

YOUR TURN:

At this moment, what one idea do you need to start executing for your business?

Question #16

What part of your business have you delegated or put on hold in order to focus your energy more efficiently?

"The question, then, is not only how to uncover our fundamental tenderness and warmth, but also how to abide there with the fragile, often bittersweet vulnerability. How can we relax and open to the uncertainty of it?"
-
Pema Chodron

Facebook, Twitter, Linked In, Digg, Stumble Upon, Delicious, Flickr, Pinterest, Google+ and so so many other "connecting" sites. Does anyone else see how ridiculous it is to think that you can be "authentic" on each AND EVERY one of these sites? I admit that for a while I would either spend half the day on these sites or use some sort of "sprinkling" method to make sure I get "exposure." But who are we kidding? If WE ARE ALL doing that, are we really connecting with anybody?

So I have scaled WAY BACK on my engagement. I love to blog, so I blog. I connect with interesting people on Twitter so I engage there as well. Lately I am addicted to YOUTUBE (I know! I am a late adopter) so I have fun over there as well. But with any engagement – yes EVEN ON Pinterest and Facebook - I am sharing and spreading the word on things I love and align with how I view life and what I want to emulate in the world. If that means I will never be a success as far as selling a bunch of "my stuff"... well after four years I guess I am good with that. I do not believe that will be the result though. I believe that one day I will find those people who find what I am saying or doing as valuable to their lives.

Paula Joerling:

The licensing part, I have an agent for that. I don't have the time or energy to send images to manufacturers, read contracts or wheel and deal. I would rather be in the studio painting.

Laura Otero:

I have learned (for myself) that taking on short term design or web projects isn't the direction that is best for my business right now. Instead, I'm focusing on longer-term clients who need help in the areas I do best. Whether that is design work, writing or social media, I'm doing what I love.

In the past, I took on most projects that came my way, even if there not a chance for repeat business. I have found that pouring my time and energy into a project (and the person, really) with no chance for long-term work hasn't been the best use of my time.

I also began to feel overwhelmed at the number of small projects and people I interacted with on such a short-term basis. When I made the decision to work with just a few clients (4 being my magic number), I felt a weight lifted and have not suffered in terms of overall project income.

The wonderful thing about this decision is that it has given me more time for art and adventures. More and more, I'm thinking about ways I could monetize my artful creations. Taking baby steps and dreaming big don't seem to go together, but I have found as long as I am moving in the right direction, I get more confident and creative along the way.

Dani Keith:

I, like most creative entrepreneurs wanted to do everything myself, it's part control and part plucky drive and while everyone, EVERYONE who is successful will tell you to delegate your weaker links to the professionals to free up your time for your strengths you still think...ahh I can handle it...well lucky for me that my other half is fluent in all things technical, so I have handed my website work to him...it is a small safety net, I know that while my husband does all of the tech work I still have complete creative control.

Phyllis Dobbs:

In my business I work on deadlines and priorities. So things that don't fit high on the priority scale at the moment get pushed back. This usually includes working on new ideas that I brainstormed and want to try out as well as technical things like upgrading software, computers and devices. I do love technology, but have to work it in.

Shari Sherman:

Although I still do 1 or 2 shows a year, I have essentially put doing outside art festivals on hold, so I can concentrate on the online side of my business more. Art festivals really helped me to become BRAVE about my art, not to mention all the wonderful people I met along the way. There is camaraderie there, and you can really develop a sense of belonging in the art community. BUT, they are a LOT of work, physical work, and I think I got kinda burned out on it. So, I decided to cut way back on that side and focus more on internet opportunities and the prospects of getting into the world of licensing.

Valerie Weller:

As of now, I am wearing all hats, since I am in the development stages of building my "art business." I suppose after the business grows more, the time will come to streamline the process, wherein I will need to delegate to an assistant.

Confession: of all the daily business tasks necessary, shipping is the one I would love to hand off first. Packing, shipping, labeling and post office are not my cup of tea. I tend to spend more time packing with love and making things look good, that I end up losing time in the day, unnecessarily. I know that once I can afford to delegate business chores, (not limited to just shipping) there would be a lot more painting and development happening.

Stephanie Guimond:

In addition to deliberately putting many ideas on hold (specific workshops & services, art shows), I've put some of the administrative parts of my business like filing and record keeping on hold while I work on developing new offerings and expanding my business platform. I'm fully aware that I can only do this for so long before it comes back to haunt me.

I intend to get help setting up a system for records and accounting - I want to work with someone who knows what they're doing to avoid major headaches come tax time. I could do the research myself, but it would take me a looooonnnnng time to figure it out because I'm just. not. that. into it. I've already spoken to someone about it last month, may this very post be my reminder to follow through!

YOUR TURN:

What part of your business have you delegated or put on hold in order to focus your energy more efficiently?

Question #17

How did you finally decide on the look of your brand? What did the evolution look like?

It's not what you look at that matters, it's what you see.

Henry David Thoreau

I have been through quite an evolution with the colors that represent my business. I have always been into funkier colors: goldenrods and burnt siennas. But since then my heart started to move toward the other end of the spectrum: clean lines with classic gray and a pop of pink. I am not really sure if the colors changed first or my take on business did. But in both places I went through a huge transformation.

After almost three years of what I call the hustle where I felt like I kept my prices too low and had a beggar's mentality about the whole business, my heart said, "you are done with this."

And I really began to ask myself:
what do I really want?
And what would it look like?

In 2012 I decided to integrate what I feel like my calling is: to work with people asking questions and offering the ear and the heart needed to witness as they come into their power. Pink is a sign of femininity. Gray is a sign of strength. Together they feel like grace.

Phyllis Dobbs:

My brand came naturally for me. First, I am pretty much obsessed with color so in everything I do, vibrant color is key. And I naturally gravitate toward whimsy. I've tried doing more traditional, but when I draw, paint and design, the whimsy comes out.

The combination of color and whimsy has defined my brand. I've had so many people tell me that my art makes them smile. That's a comment that makes me smile and happy with what I do.

Paula Joerling:

That was a difficult thing to do. I started by looking at lots of blogs and websites to see what other people had done. After determining what I liked about their brand, I took the time to understand what it said about them and how it related to their work.

Next I selected some of my favorite images based on what I wanted to say about the work that I did. That was tricky because I like doing a lot of different things and I needed them to all make sense together.

The next step was to show it to a couple of different friends (both artists and non-artists) and get feedback.

Dani Keith:

My work is very personal, my jewelry is an expression of my joy and as a creative your work is always very closely tied to who you are…that notion speaks directly to my branding… as a designer my product is always evolving, the ring I make today is nothing like what I will make in a month and I always like to offer original work to my clients… so my name is the continuity to my craft, and that is the evolution of
the {dani keith designs} brand.

Shari Sherman:

My brand is still a work in progress. I am from Hawaii and I live in Florida and love the beach, so that is how I arrived at my island style! I am working on a logo for Hula Dog Designs. I think branding should reflect both your personality and your business, and I want to create a brand that says whimsical, fun and relaxed...what is more fun than a dog in a hula skirt?

Stephanie Guimond:

I don't have a firm or final look for my brand yet. With each evolution of my blog/Website I play around with the look & feel to reach something that feels right and captures what I want to project: a look that's grounded and vibrant where the left and right sides of the brain meet.

I do like what I have now look-wise (with a few tweaks). I'm in the process of creating a new Website and tried switching it up with something different; though visually I loved the end result it just didn't feel right so I'll continue with the look I have now at the new URL and see how that sits.

In addition to visual aspects of branding I've been paying attention to the voice I use across social platforms and in person when representing my business, as well as the consistency of my message. My first blog was purely narrative and used to document a key personal transition with no intent to drum up business. Though I still include some personal narrative, today I use my blog to support my business vision and that's narrowed the focus of my writings considerably.

Laura Otero:

My marketing blog, business website, personal blog, Facebook page and Twitter account all have a unified look. This was a definite process for me, even though I'm a designer! I decided on red, white and black as my business colors. I didn't want anything too girly, and felt black and white were crisp and professional enough to make both men and women feel comfortable on my blog.

When I first started my blogging and business, I went with a navy and light blue color scheme, and more girly fonts. Over time, I felt like I wanted something that felt more like "me."

Especially with us creative folks, we have a tendency to redesign our online spaces and logos more often than others. Even though it's been less than a year, I'm already ready to change things up! I have to remember (as a marketer) that branding myself is a process, and that is isn't always the best decision to change things just when people have come to recognize and know me by the colors and look I've established.

I have also learned to not be so hard on myself. Even artists with huge followings often have their blogs on a simple blogspot site, with pretty customizations. As long as the content is high quality and it's written from the heart, I have to believe readers won't know or even care about where the blog is hosted. Another one of my favorites is
"A Beautiful Mess" blog – another example of a simple blog platform customized in a way that is allows the artist to shine.

YOUR TURN:

How did you finally decide on the look of your brand? What did the evolution look like?

Question #18

Who is that one person you would like to sit and talk with about your business? What would you talk about?

> *Life is pure adventure, and the sooner we realize that, the quicker we will be able to treat life as art.*
>
> *Maya Angelou*

So the first person that came to my mind is Danielle LaPorte. Pretty much everything I read that she puts out into the world is a direct challenge to me to:

Move. Grow. Think. Trust. Believe. Launch and Learn. Begin Again.

In other words, she cuts through the B.S. And not in this pie in the sky way. She is not telling me to quit my day job and go for my dreams. She is challenging to think about the motives behind that and then once I am clear about that, begin to do a little more of what I want to do and a little less of what I do not want to do. Practical, right?

But here is the thing. If I were able to gain an audience with her, the last thing I would want to do is talk. She could pretty much take any of her talks and maybe add to it based on her present experiences. Because for me repetition is good.

Phyllis Dobbs:

I am in a huge network of people with the same type of business as mine. So I would go in a different direction. Tony Ford is the one I would love to sit and talk with. I think of him as a tech guru for social media. I have attended several of Tony's seminars and came away with so much information. He is very up to date with all of it. In today's world, social media is so important for business so I would discuss the rapidly changing world of social media and technology and how to use it effectively with my business. I would also like to know more on how to work with the Panda Slap, which I didn't know existed until the last seminar I attended of his. (Tony Ford is the COO of ArtFire.com and the Technology Expert for the Craft and Hobby Association, CHA).

Shari Sherman:

I would like to sit and talk with Oprah! That would be a dream come true! Hopefully, we would talk about how super successful I am and how I am part of a phenomenon of artists who are spilling their hearts, following their inklings, and changing the world for the better!

Laura Otero:

I'd love to sit and talk with Kelly Rae Roberts. Having followed her blog for years, I signed up for her "Flying Lessons" course over two years ago and loved it. She has inspired so many "flyers" from all around the world. I feel like I found my creative "tribe" online through Kelly. We have a Facebook group where we connect, and have since followed each other's blogs and twitter accounts.

What I love about Kelly most is… Her belief in herself, her gorgeous art, and her inspiring quotes painted into her work, her spirit, and her writing/blogging.

What would we talk about? I'd ask her to share her dream-to-life process. For example, how does she know what direction to take her art biz? I'm sure it's part-heart and part-biz savvy, but I'd love to know the process from start to finish! I'd also ask her how she structures her day in terms of art and blogging/biz computer stuff. I try to write my blog posts in blocks, but they don't always feel as inspiring to me that way.

I'd ask her what the one thing is that she would have done differently over the past few years. I have a tendency to take on too much at once, and I have noticed she also works very, very hard. She taught the first Flying Lessons class when she was very pregnant and moving! Does she regret pushing herself so hard, or is it necessary to grow the biz? I'm learning to take more time for self-care and quiet time, which is why I'm curious.

Then I would thank her from the bottom of my heart for being such an inspiring force for so many of us creatives!

Valerie Weller:

If we are referring to the here and now…I'd love to sit down and chat with Flora Bowley and Kelly Rae Roberts together. I've been influenced by both of these dynamic women through several recent courses I've taken, that a chat would be invaluable. I'd be most interested in learning more about Flora's business story, and how she was able to position herself to teach, create, and travel as the foundation of what she does. With Kelly, I'd be most interested in discussing my art direction and her thoughts on my "art transition" in business. Between both of these ladies, I know I'd gather some very fruitful advice.

And of course… (this is how my mind thinks…) if we are talking about a person that has passed, I'd be way excited to speak to

Sergeant, Sorolla, or Cezanne about painting and color. Just have to cover all bases.

Dani Keith:

I feel as though I am the luckiest of creatives in that the giants of my artisan jewelry world are very accessible. I have bench space with Ginger Meek Allen and have had the recent pleasure to meet with and talk to Ken Bova. Both artists create a life based on their art and make exceptional artisan jewelry.

Having people who talk about establishing a creative life without the notion of being a starving artist is so vital. I also believe that is so essential to seek out the people in your sphere that have taken their art/craft to the next level that you aspire too and reach out...most people in our lines of work are very generous with their knowledge and time.

Stephanie Guimond:

Only one person? Gosh.
I think I'll have to go with Tara Gentile, I respect the expertise she can offer. I'd love to chat about what next steps and/or products would yield the greatest potential for income relatively quickly, pricing, and how & where to best engage with my target market. While we're at it, I'd also love to hear about her core business model and strategic planning process.

Paula Joerling:

A magic genie. Seriously though, I have been "in the business" as they say, a long time and I pretty much get to talk to all of the people that I want to talk to. I am very fortunate to have an amazing network of creative, successful and sharing friends.

YOUR TURN:

Who is that one person you would like to sit and talk with about your business? What would you talk about?

Question #19

What is one activity within your business that you incorporate on a regular basis that reminds you of the value of what you are doing?

Take chances, make mistakes. That's how you grow. Pain nourishes your courage. You have to fail in order to practice being brave.

-
Mary Tyler Moore

Morning quiet time.

The early morning hours are when I am most fresh. At the same time, the morning time is when I wake up with a laundry list of what I need to take care of. Sometimes the list feels so overwhelming I think I should 'chuck' the morning quiet time. I think that will easily give me a 30 minute jump start on my to-do list.

Here's the problem though. Those 20-30 minutes every morning gives me a fresh perspective, helps me prioritize my day, reminds me that my heart and my work is in God's hands. As I remind myself that I am a vessel for the soulful work that comes through me, it reminds me to not get anxious over such things as did I 'tweet' the links enough, how many fans on Facebook do I have, the work is for those who I am meant to meet and connect with and vice versa.

Lisa Wilson:

Listening. Open, receptive listening.

I started blogging several years ago, and immediately became attached to the feedback. If I didn't get a comment, I would wonder for days what was wrong with the post! I watched my follower numbers incessantly, hitting "refresh" sometimes just to see if something happened in the past 2 minutes. That type of attachment wore me out quickly.

As I started to take LifeUnity to a different sphere, one driven by my voice instead of the echo, I had to release my attachment to comments and numbers and praise and criticism. But in so doing, I also hardened myself to the kinder words – those that were honestly reflecting back to me the value I was giving to others. I didn't know how to handle the negative feedback alongside the positive feedback without becoming derailed by it all. To silence the critical voices in my mind, I detached myself from all comments on my work. I just stopped listening.

Over the past year or so, I've started listening again. And what I hear amazes me. I started telling the truth (the whole truth, and nothing but the truth), and people responded. Not to some false message I was trying to get out there or fancy title built to garner SEO ratings, but to my unique, honest voice. And not only did they respond, but I started to see changes in their lives as well. Mindful moments in which they connected with their children, art projects inspired by something I'd said, revelations about their own lives based on some phrase I'd left in a comment...

When I look around the internet, when I go out shopping and just listen to the conversations that are happening, I hear so much pain and suffering. And when I offer words of encouragement and inspiration through my site and my art, I hear the way people respond. I hear how, if even for a moment, they see how a life of less pain is possible.

I cannot tell you how much those simple moments fill me with unlimited energy to keep doing what I'm doing and being who I am. All because I listened.

Katie Clemons:

I journal and embellish my journals a lot. Sometimes when you turn a hobby into a career, you don't want to do it for fun anymore. But that's not the case with journaling. I'm more inspired than ever to document my story. I see more and more how no one else can write my story. I see how reflecting on my story gives me more gratitude and happiness in life.

It inspires me to want to help women with their storykeeping more and more, too.

Kat Sloma:

I seek feedback from the participants of my classes in surveys as a class completes. Seeing comments like, "I learned so much more than I expected from this class" or "I am more confident in myself and my photography," gives me warm fuzzies. It reminds me why I do what I do!

Julene Ewert:

Each month I send out an email to friends and customers and I post to my blog. My idea is to connect with my people personally, not just push the next new item for sale. I always try to send out into the world a message that has meaning to me - I make a point of being my true self. I tell stories from my heart, typically sharing inspirations from my travels.

For example, I recently posted upon returning from the Oregon coast that "...The view was breathtaking. Moments like these remind me to take time to breathe. Most of the time I am working far into the future. Yes, it seems I'm constantly rushing towards the next goal or deadline - designing Christmas cards in February...creating art that will be used on next year's calendar." Along with these thoughts I posted a picture of my son, on his back with his legs in the air, laughing hysterically holding on to his kite string for dear life. What I said was that "My hope is to do more of this...to take a moment each day to just BE in that moment. Because moments like these are fleeting and precious.

I communicate through my business like I'm talking to my best friend. It's rewarding for me to share a part of my life with others, and the best part is it is easy to be myself.

Jodi Lebrun:

Gratitude. Without a doubt. I am thankful every day for the women that buy my jewelry, sign up for my e-courses, ask for a reading or allow me to send them healing energy. I thank each and every one of them silently and via email for the opportunity to provide them with what they need in that moment. It is my life's passion to help women to re-connect with their minds, bodies and spirits and each time I get to do this, saying thank you is the least I can do.

Erin Fickert-Rowland:

Blogging is an activity that I have come to cherish, because it keeps me accountable to my business and connected to my customers. A blog is such a versatile and indispensible tool. I use it to report on local activities, educate on Art trends and techniques, empower personal and family creativity, and to regularly challenge myself to grow and explore new skills.

My blog allows me to keep in constant contact with my family, friends, customers, and new acquaintances, especially as I feed my posts through other social media outlets. It is highly rewarding to see certain blog posts take off in popularity, and to hear from others how I have inspired or encouraged them. My blog is also one of the most tangible ways I can look back to see my business' growth and progression. The capability to store and view projects from years ago provides me with motivation to continually improve, and the ability to recognize how far I have come!

Louise Gale:

I really like to plan out activities and milestones for both my business and for myself so one of the activities I incorporate is to take a step back every month, see where I am and what activities or goals I'd like to meet the following month. This is a great way to celebrate what I have accomplished and then focus my business and activities going forward. Reflecting often helps me stay present with what I love, enjoy every moment and plan the next steps.

Kim Gann:

I Dream. I wish I could say blogging, but that is really hard for me. I try to paint everyday.

Laura Gaffke:

Collaboration is an extremely valued practice in my business. I have an ongoing, collaborative, creative practice and blog with my friend and fellow artist, Tina Hirsig called "lauraTWOtina". Our work together stretches me in ways that I don't think I would have otherwise and reminds me of why I am creating the work I am. Tina is like a positive mirror gently prompting me to go deeper, ask more questions and try new things, all while reminding me to be true to myself. She values my work and although I think everyone needs a cheerleader she is more than that. She is my business partner, touchstone, confident, goal setter and benchmark for staying on track.

I also helped create an Art Salon that consists of creative women in my local community. Our group is alive with a diverse group of artists, including photographers, collage and mixed media artists, as well as painters. We affectionately call ourselves "Salonistas" and get together regularly with the intention of sharing resources, giving feedback, making professional connections and simply enjoying an evening with interesting friends. We grow together through the accountability of goal setting both in our creative work as well as in our businesses. We all value and support each other, sharing our triumphs, struggles and individual expertise. When one of us achieves a goal like having a solo show, getting a grant, opening an online shop or creating new work it motivates us and propels us forward in our own work. Great things can be achieved in with the support of others and I am grateful for so many innovative, caring, thoughtful friends.

Juliette Crane:

Creating art. When I first started my business, I let painting slide because it felt like a luxury and I thought the business side needed to come first.

Over time, I've remembered that the reason I started my creative business is because I love to create. Painting and sharing my process and techniques are my passion. If I don't do them on a regular basis for myself, I get frustrated and unbalanced and that means my life and business don't thrive.

I also now see that I wouldn't have a business to begin with if it wasn't for my creativity. So I remember this whenever I think I "should" be doing one thing, but really feel the need to create and always give myself time to paint.

Carrie Schmidt:

Sharing my art with others and engaging in art-inspired conversations. One such moment occurred when I participated in my first outdoor art festival a few weeks ago, and it was life changing. Witnessing how others reacted joyfully to my art was fulfilling and made me realize the value in what I am doing. I was especially touched by the children's heartfelt reactions.
One girl looked at me with huge eyes and said, "You are so amazing." She begged her mom to buy a painting for her room, and her mother acquiesced. I love that this little girl wanted an original piece of artwork in a time of mass produced everything. (She is a future Etsy shopper for sure!)

I was surprised by how much this meant to me and how it inspired me to keep creating. I love talking to these children about art and how they are artists too. I think there is value in being an example for these kids. Anyone who chooses to be an artist is brave because it is not a profession that is very encouraged, nor is it even seen as a necessarily valuable way to spend time. There is also value in debunking the myth that only certain people are artists. I love to talk to children and adults about how we are all creative beings by our very essence of being human.

I love the quote,

> "Don't ask what the world needs. Ask what makes you come alive, and go do it. Because what the world needs are people who have come alive."

I feel that I am a better person because I am following my authentic path—a path where I can't sleep at night because I'm so excited to paint the next morning, so excited to explore the world to find beauty. This means to me that there is value in everything I do related to art.

Elizabeth Gonzalez:

I make a list, written or in my mind, of words of encouragements I have received or about people that has been inspired with my work or who told me that my work made them smile.

Amanda Fall:

I'm blessed to work with dozens of amazing artists, writers, and creatives of all kinds throughout the production of Sprout, my online magazine. Interacting with this "tribe" of kindred spirits and working together to inspire others—well, I can't imagine anything better! Every time someone writes to tell me that Sprout has encouraged or helped them, I am flooded with gratitude for this work (which is really my mission).

Sprout is all about connection—with contributors, with readers, with this amazing world we live in. Connection is what keeps me going every day.

E'Layne Koenigsberg:

Writing...funny answer for an artist. I write almost all my own sayings that I put on my art...I love words...playing with words...painting pictures with words...evoking emotions with words. Women (and a few brave men) come into the booth and the sayings speak to them...they are personal and many times profound. I've had women burst out in tears and tell me what they have read went to the core of their being, empowered them and stirred change. That makes my heart sing!

Beth Doan:

Donating my work for local charity events. Although my intention is to one day make a living full time from my Art, my Art is way more than that. It is not just about money. It is who I am and I love sharing it & paying it forward with my Art.

Liv Lane:

I keep a "love notes" folder in my email where I hang onto meaningful messages from blog readers, art buyers and e-course students. Occasionally, when I need a lift, I'll browse through old notes to be reminded why I do what I do and how it serves others. That fills me up.

Mandy Saile:

Being with animals and snuggling with my rabbits is something I do every single day, no matter what I have going on in the studio or no matter how busy I may be. My rabbit snuggling time is key to keeping me on track to feeling positive, joyful, and inspired about life and that bleeds right into the artwork I want to create. The rabbits are quick reminders to work hard and to stay true to myself, no matter what because hopefully if I do so then I'll eventually find my dream niches and hit my target market and all of the super great opportunities will happen which will lead right into my being able to open my long dreamt of rabbit sanctuary/rescue.

 I also find that keeping an activity log is a really good thing for me to continually do. On those days where I am feeling down on myself and on my progress, etc I can look at my activity log and say 'Hey look at all you've done this past month, your trying, it's okay, just keep on moving ahead, keep on trying," for that's all you can do at the end of the day, the only thing you can't really fail at is trying your hardest.

Sticky notes are a regular part of my studio day as well, ha ha. I have a huge calendar on my desk and it's jam packed with stick-it notes, just tons of things I want to try or get done, places I want to submit and apply to, and projects I want to get done. Everything goes on a stick-it note and then they are scattered throughout the calendar months in what I feel is a reasonable time schedule. This routine is key for me lately because on those days where I think 'oh I can take it easy, there's not much to do…' or on those days where I am feeling like I've tried it all, nothing is working, and I am wondering where do I go from here? One glance at the calendar full of stick-it notes reminds me that there is lots to do, so there is no reason to be idle and that there are still lots of routes and doors to try.

Also, as a severe acute and chronic migraine sufferer, the stick-it notes system allows me to easily move items and to-do things to another day, week or another month on those days where I fight my hardest but my time is cut short due to the head pain. I do admit that I always wonder, just where my business would be these days if I were one of the very lucky ones who don't suffer from migraines but then again my head pain has really forced me to slow down and take in extraordinary beauty and appreciation for life, so I can never be sorry for that.

YOUR TURN:

What is one activity within your business that you incorporate on a regular basis that reminds you of the value of what you are doing?

Question #20

What tools have you used to streamline the necessary "evils" of your business?

> *Every great dream begins with a dreamer. Always remember, you have within you the strength, the patience, and the passion to reach for the stars to change the world.*
>
> *Harriet Tubman*

Hootsuite is such a great resource to keep me organized with social media. You are able to link all your social media sites, schedule your posting days in advance and helps you to keep up with who is connecting with you.

Lisa Wilson:

I allow myself small steps in a constant flow of activity without getting attached to or overwhelmed by any one action.

I have many time-consuming aspects of my business, many behind-the-scenes activities that are necessary to keep the business running but that aren't necessarily "fun." If I find myself dreading a to-do, not only am I less likely to begin doing it, but the actual process becomes almost painful. If I keep taking one small step at a time – opening the inbox, clicking on the first email, etc. – without letting myself get caught up in my feelings about doing so, I find myself moving much more efficiently and, perhaps most important, in a far more peaceful manner.

In addition, once I find myself starting to become overwhelmed, I take the next small step on a different project ...or several small steps outside, away from the computer or studio, and into nature.

Catherine Just:

I hired a team to help me. I learned early on that if I don't delegate I won't leverage my business. I cannot do everything and still innovate and create. I needed experts to support me by doing what they do best so that I could do what I do best.

Kat Sloma:

I try to create systems. If I am doing something over and over, I test out the best way to do the task and then document it for myself. There is nothing worse than doing a task every few months and forgetting how to do it! By creating and using notes, I save time.

I also use the right tools for the job. I have an organizer for planning, spreadsheets for tracking, and use dedicated software for accounting and list management. Using the right tool for a task streamlines activities. I don't need to reinvent the wheel for things like accounting! It takes some upfront investment to investigate, purchase and learn a tool but the time and energy saved in the long run is worth it.

Julene Ewert:

The drudgery of accounting is tough for me. Not only is the whole concept a bit daunting, it has never been an activity that I've looked forward to. When I first started my business, I used an Excel spreadsheet to keep track of sales and inventory. After the first years of calculating and re-calculating, and sifting through stacks of receipts, I decided that I needed a much better system - one I could do on my own. I dove into the computer program Quickbooks. It took a good deal of effort, a few classes, and a bit of seat-of-the-pants experimentation - but I'm proud to say that an artist like me can run it. I actually find it fun to "run" the reports to see which products are contributing most to my sales. Plus, it's now so easy to prepare for tax time. I no longer dread this necessary part of running my own business - and I actually get some joy from it!

Jodi Lebrun:

With the launch of Where The Spirited Women Gather, my inbox gets pretty full now with emails that I can't forget about. Using the Flag feature within my email program helps me to not lose any. I also have my Facebook business page linked to my Twitter account so that anything I post there is automatically tweeted without me having to switch over to Twitter. I use a bulletin board to pin up any forms that I will be needing and I keep a giant sketchbook beside me at all times so that I can write down any tasks that need to be done. It's probably my favorite tool as I doodle in it, brainstorm in it and know to check it regularly

Erin Fickert-Rowland:

In my opinion, there are two big "evils" involved with being an artist working in multiple mediums in the Web 2.0 world: 1) **preparing photographs for an online presence**, and 2) **maintaining an organized studio**. To streamline my ability to share my work and activities online, I have found my iPhone, Adobe Photoshop, and Flickr to be absolutely essential tools. To maintain order and increase the efficiency of my time in the studio, I cannot live without clear Sterilite Containers and my Dymo Label Maker!

Louise Gale:

Recently I have been on a mission to simplify my business (and my life!). It's not necessarily an evil, but I do have a lot of ideas and sometimes I can get myself overwhelmed, as I want to do all of them! So I use a lot of visionboarding to help me focus my energies and take time out if I find myself procrastinating!

Juliette Crane:

I've learned I have left and right brained moments. I used to fight the two sides and have a to-do list every day. I'd make myself create when I really wanted to do something that was more organized and had an answer (like photographing art for my online shop or writing a blog post). Or I would make my creative side wait so I could follow up on the business side of things.

Now I take advantage of my moods, keeping in mind what I need to accomplish overall, but I've found not trying to force myself into a box of task-accomplishing or creating on-demand makes me, my business and life more balanced and helps keep me in alignment with my long-term goals.

I'm a very disciplined person and thrive with a bit of routine, so not having a strict to-do list works best for me. I never have trouble keeping myself on task because I'm always feeling I should be doing something. I have a harder time giving myself a break, but I've learned that of course helps everything flow better too.

I also schedule blog posts, social media (via HootSuite) and whatever I can in advance, so I can utilize what I feel like doing in the moment and still accomplish what I need to get done overall.

I compartmentalize tasks, especially non-creative things I don't always adore doing like tasks related to shop updates, packaging orders, photographing artwork, restocking supplies, and do those tasks when I feel like it all at once, but without pressure. I used to tell myself if I was doing a shop update I had to include every single piece of new artwork and then make sure each was included in my newsletter. It all became a big task I never wanted to do and I always avoided. Not being so hard on myself and knowing it's okay to do things in phases and at my own pace has made everything much more enjoyable.

Elizabeth Gonzalez:

Delegate what I don't like or make me feel bored. I also incorporated tools to make things easier and productive. For example, I made stamps and cutters for a few details in my ceramic pieces. Another strategy is split the different tasks in short periods of time making the job easier and less boring.

Amanda Fall:

Honestly? I'm still working on that! I'm a "real paper" person, which is ironic, since my business is strictly online (although Sprout's style incorporates lots of handmade work). I surround myself with Post-its and notes scribbled on whatever was handy (I've been known to use napkins and junk mail in a pinch). Aside from my "real" written notes, I use lots of folders on my laptop to sort and prioritize. Gmail's search function saves me on a daily basis!

E'Layne Koenigsberg:

I don't know if you can consider an accountant a "tool" but I'm all about hiring people to do the things I don't love to do.

Beth Doan:

This is a work in progress for me. I have lots of streamlining ideas, that I know would work and would be really helpful to me, but after working all day as Administrative Assistant, it's hard to get the paintbrush out of my hand and do more Administrative type work at home.

Liv Lane:

Well, I've learned to delegate much of the stuff that wears me out, distracts me or I'm just not good at. I have an assistant who takes care of behind-the-scenes details in my Etsy shop, like handling shipping and sourcing supplies. I love creating and marketing my art, but I was so relieved to take those other details off my plate. I have an awesome web master {Michele Bergh} who fixes things in minutes that would have taken me hours to figure out. I have a great tax accountant who gives me good guidance and watches out for my business. I still work a ton, but it's on the stuff I know and love while trusting the peeps in my corner that are doing what they know and love.

Mandy Saile:

Positive thinking is a necessary tool, I believe. Being positive, having hope and believing that my unique and kind spirit flows right into all of the artwork that I make is something I hold strongly to and that I know no one can take away from me and in the end that gives me strength to continue through any struggle or evil of the business.

YOUR TURN:

What tools have you used to streamline the necessary "evils" of your business?

Question #21

How do you go about keeping a sense of "wonder" in your business?

> *I slept and dreamt that life was joy.*
> *I awoke and saw that life was service.*
> *I acted and behold, service was joy.*
>
> Rabindranath Tagore

I make sure to have creative time every day. I do this by coming up with projects that keep it scheduled into my day. One way I have done it in the past is to join a couple of flickr sites of mixed media artists and connect with them via their blogs to help me stay connected to the 'art' side of creativity rather than constantly being about the business side.

Right now I am in the middle of a mail art project called the Spark and Inspire Project. The goal is to send out 100 one of a kind projects and I should be finished by the end of 2012.

Lisa Wilson:

Without wonder, my business wouldn't exist! As an Awareness Artist, a foundational practice is awareness (broadening or focusing mindful perspective). In practicing awareness, I am constantly opening myself to the wonders of the world and of this moment.

As in my life, so in my business.

If I find myself getting bored or losing interest, I simply re-adjust my perspective. In practical terms this means I delve into another component of my business that I perhaps haven't visited in awhile – like acrylic painting, finding new blogs or organizations, or sending out some emails to those with whom I haven't been in recent contact. Or, I'll get out of the house and venture out to take photos or have lunch with someone to discuss art or business ethics. While engaged with my art, I'll turn a piece upside-down, take it to view in a different light, or put on a different type of music to see how it influences and changes my views on the piece.

This change of perspective, while staying focused on my overall messages of awareness, always brings a fresh sense of wonder to the process.

Catherine Just:

I am very curious and love to research things pertaining to business, so owning my own business allows me to keep learning and growing. I take a lot of online classes to help me keep learning and remind me I am not going it alone, and I seek out mentors that have something to share that inspires me.

Kat Sloma:

First, I practice my own art. All of the "wonder" that feeds my business comes from my own practice of art and creativity. If I'm not being creative, exploring the world with my camera and discovering new things for myself, I am going to lose touch with why I started my business in the first place. I am going to lose the personal and artistic growth of my own journey, which becomes the source of inspiration for my classes.

Second, I listen to my heart. There are times that I start down a path that seems like a good business opportunity only to find that I am not excited for the direction I am heading. I have to stay aligned with my heart to keep my excitement, or the "wonder" is lost. My brain may tell me that something is a perfectly good business opportunity and I should go for it, but if my heart is telling me it's not right, or I don't feel any excitement about it, I won't pursue it.

When I am creating, growing and staying aligned with my heart everything seems to flow naturally. The "wonder" is there!

Julene Ewert:

I feel that everyday is a gift. Okay, that sounds a bit corny, but it's is completely true. Each day I have the opportunity to explore the unknown. I truly love thinking up a new product, from how it will be made to the final packaging and presentation.

I take the same approach with my artwork. There are so many ways to approach a single idea. There is no single correct choice - you have to wonder..."what if I...?" This keeps me engaged, and keeps a sense of wonder to creating something new.

If you ever think you've lost your sense of "wonder" have a conversation with a small child. They have wonder burning deep within them - and we need to do our best to not extinguish their sincere sense of wonder, or ours. I love this!

Jodi Lebrun:

My whole business is centered on 'wonder.' Keeping this feeling alive and well is the best part of what I do. Each time I perform a long-distance healing session or do an oracle card reading for a client, I get to experience the magic of the Universe and all that it encompasses. I also have the luxury, if I'm not feeling the 'wonder', to reach out to one of the many women in my Spirited Women's Circle and ask her how she's doing or if she needs anything. Just by tuning in to another human being, I'm reminded how amazing life really is.

Erin Fickert-Rowland:

I always have my nose in as many Art/Craft books as possible (and I have the library fines to prove it!) I want to know what modern material and techniques are available, and I am continually learning how to use as many of them as possible to incorporate into my work. When you realize your tools can perform multiple tasks, or you can manipulate an art supply for an entirely new function- that maintains a healthy sense of wonder!

Visiting as many local art shows and museum exhibits as I can also inspires my sense of wonder. I am fascinated by artists and the brilliant ways they can uniquely express themselves through their work. Constantly learning about artists, past and present, reinvigorates my sense of wonder and reminds me that the possibilities are limitless.

Louise Gale:

I am constantly finding inspiration through other creative souls, websites, blogs and observing the natural world. I do practice living in the moment as much as I can to keep life simple and beautiful. There is so much wonder in the everyday so I do keep that sense of wonder in that present moment and enjoy those little bursts of inspiration.

Kim Gann:

I am constantly creating new collections and trying new approaches in business.

Cindy Silverstein:

Wonder is a sense of excitement, enthusiasm and delight. These qualities are essential to my business and exist at its core. My business is a reflection of myself. It is a living creation that arises out of my attitudes and beliefs, which form the foundation that my business is built upon, and that is true even if I am not conscious of it. I believe that it is important, even crucial, in life as well as in business that I observe my attitudes, thoughts, and feelings in order to foster an inner environment that is uplifting, loving, and affirming, especially toward myself. This can be a real challenge, and at times it can even seem unachievable. I am often very critical of myself, more so than of others. When I take time for reflection, journaling, contemplation, reading inspiring works, meditation, yoga, or walking, the negativities that I absorb from the world outside and from my own negative thoughts are cleared away. When my mind is clear of these distractions, it is easy for the sense of wonder to naturally spring to the surface.

Being around nature and animals brings me in touch with a more authentic and natural part of myself and the wisdom of great teachers remind me to keep my outlook fresh, positive and full of wonder. This sense of wonder fuels the connection that I have with my work, and helps me to remember the reason that I make art. I want to be able to see the inner beauty and greatness in myself. Only then will I see these qualities in everyone.

My goal in life over the past 35 years has been to live consciously, to be aware of how everything I do, what I think, and what I say, have a profound effect on my life and my world. This belief has led me to fine tune and elevate my inner as well as my outer environments. My creativity and my creations are a reflection of the beliefs and attitudes I hold inside. I believe that a sense of wonder in business manifests naturally out of a love and respect toward all of life.

Laura Gaffke:

I find that making time for myself to reflect, sketch and write is an intricate part of my business. Walks in the woods or at the beach free my mind and allow room for new ideas to take form. I often walk with my iPhone and use the voice memo feature to record ideas as they come to me so I don't have to worry about remembering them and I can just allow my thoughts to flow. There have been so many times I thought I would remember that "brilliant" idea and then didn't so this has been working great for me.

I also do this in my journal, a practice I learned from Julia Cameron's "The Artist's Way" which encourages stream of consciousness writing. This along with painting centers me. It gets me out of my "research mode" where I can often pay too much attention to what "everyone else" is doing instead of listening to my own "inner guides." From here I can grow my business in a way that is authentic to me.

Juliette Crane:

I consistently develop new products and communicate with students and customers. I used to find wonder in the idea that my artwork would be published on calendars and journals that could be sold at book stores. Over time, I realized that wasn't really what lights my fire. For me, it's really about diving into and sharing my unique gifts with the world.

For me, it's about finding ways to take what I love and what I am passionate about and enjoy doing and using that to help, encourage and inspire others. That's what keeps me going every day and knowing that I can have an idea and put it out there for the world to be nourished by and seeing just how those ideas, my artwork, my business and the amazing people around me evolve is a crazy sense of wonder.

Carrie Schmidt:

By seeking and connecting with others who inspire me, as well as experiences that move me. I live for those moments of serendipity, and by allowing myself to be more vulnerable I am opening myself up to more of them.
I like to explore new places and put myself in new situations where my senses are heightened and stimulated.

Whenever I'm stuck or feeling a little un-inspired, trying something new brings me back to a state of wonder, which leads to excitement that seems to re-energize and inspire me. Creating is always a new experience, so it is easy to sustain the wonder in it for me.

Mary Nasser:

To keep a sense of wonder in my work, I am continually learning. I love to learn!

My curiosity usually gets the best of me as I experiment with incorporating new materials and techniques into my artwork. I also enjoy studying and researching topics foreign to me like geology. Traveling is one of my passions and is always a learning experience as well. In my free time, I like taking art workshops and online classes on blogging, too.

In addition, it's fulfilling for me to use my art talents to be of service to others, whether it's offering free art therapy workshops at hospitals or volunteering on the board of St. Louis' chapter of Women's Caucus for Art or creating sculptures for auctions to benefit the Humane Society, Wings, or the APA of Missouri . All of these combined help me keep a sense of wonder and energizes me.

Amanda Fall:

Ahh, here's the real beauty. One of the reasons Sprout has been so successful for me is that I get to incorporate so many of my loves into its production and development. Talking a photo-walk? Research! Playing with paint? Creating backgrounds. Bouncing around the 'net for inspiration? Scouting new talent. Every day is an adventure with Sprout. I am never bored.

E'Layne Koenigsberg:

Creativity is pure magic to me...and everything we do in business is about creating something from an idea. My mind creates 24/7 and I guess it was just built that way. I've always felt that creating art...or creating anything... is more of a co-creation...there is a higher power or a plain where great ideas and inspiration exist and if we remain open to "it"... "it" flows through us into manifestation.

The details of growing a business are a bit more challenging!! The joy of creating keeps me plugging away with the more mundane parts of the business world. Taking online classes and always learning helps enormously with the sense of wonder and excitement.

Katherine Quinn:

I think sometimes I slip into my children's world and see things through their eyes, or find memories from my own childhood.

Beth Doan:

I am fortunate that since I can remember my brain is continually creating. I often fall asleep painting in my head. So, the process of blank canvas or surface to completed Art Work or taking a treasure from the ocean/beach and transform it into something else, humbles me every time. When it's done and I step back and look at the finished project, I think, where did that come from?

Liv Lane:

Ohh, good question! I guess it comes down to gratitude and delight. When a new opportunity arises or a project is going well, I revel in it. I share it with my husband or other loved ones, I whisper thanks to the powers that be, and when I'm feeling overloaded, I remind myself that the alternative is sitting in a cubicle on someone else's time doing someone else's work. Right away, I feel so grateful for the path I've taken and the things I've learned along the way.

Mandy Saile:

I think I am just a person who finds so much beauty in every day and this helps to keep the wonder alive and kicking. I feel so very blessed to be an artist, to be able to do it full-time at the present, I don't take any day for granted, especially with the migraines I endure. Art time is almost always such a huge treat and that creates wonder in itself I suppose. I also know that I have a very natural sense of wonder and I think that just bleeds into my business naturally.

As for artwork itself, I am a multi-media artist. I get bored just sticking to one medium and one series all of the time and I pride myself on being super creative and having each piece completely different from the next…that takes real creativity. I make sure I am not a 'cookie-cutter' artist and I work on several different pieces, series and mediums all at once, so constantly changing it up helps me keep up a wonderment of the art world and all it has to offer up.

YOUR TURN:

How do you go about keeping a sense of "wonder" in your business?

Question #22

In the Book: The Big Leap" by Gay Hendricks, he distinguishes between two zones that we work within: the zone of excellence and the zone of genius. Hendricks says to find true fulfillment in your work, you need to work in your zone of genius. How do you respond to this assertion and how are you experiencing this within your business?

Hope begins in the dark, the stubborn hope that if you just show up and try to do the right thing, the dawn will come. You wait and watch and work: you don't give up.

-

Anne Lamott

I agree that the zone of genius is the most effective place to really connect with the voice of your business but I do find it very scary to stay in that zone. That zone does not tend to offer quick results monetarily and I find myself wanting to fall back into the excellence zone of my 'hustle' – my comfort space.

The problem? It does not leave much energy for the projects that are my core mission. So it has been an incredible and not so easy struggle for me over the last four years to stay in the zone I KNOW I need to be in.

Lisa Wilson:

I'm not really sure what he means by 'excellence' and 'genius'. Words can be very loaded – both in meaning and in connotation.

For me, both words (excellence & genius) create a sense of expectation. Fulfillment itself becomes some elusive goal. Working in my 'zone of genius' feels as though there is some place I need to be and some way of working that I need to do if I am to be fulfilled through my work. I tend to practice a more Zen-like approach where there is nowhere else to be, nothing else to do, and no other way to be doing it.

I find true fulfillment (in the sense of peaceful existence) when I just am. If I am trying to do something better, make a piece of art look a certain way, or finish x number of things before the kids get off of the bus – no matter how passionate I am or how 'in the zone of genius' I might be, I'm not present for my experience. I'm not in peace. I'm not fulfilled.

Kat Sloma:

I haven't read the book, but if I interpret this idea for myself, I would say the "zone of genius" would be where you are doing something that is truly unique to you, your passion, while the "zone of excellence" is where you may be doing something that others also do, even if you are doing it really well.

From the standpoint of my photography classes, I am in my "zone of genius" when I create from my personal experiences and take a unique point of view. The classes come from my own journey. My classes are unique for photography classes, they tap into the heart and ask participants to look inside themselves as much as look at the world around them. The classes do not provide a formula; they ask participants to take their own stance and make their own decisions. They increase the participants' internal confidence, which is ultimately reflected in their artistic work. This is incredibly fulfilling!

Contrast this with most photography classes available, which are technical classes. They are the "how to" type of classes. Use these settings, in this situation, to get this result. I could teach technical classes because I know and understand the technical part in order to create my art, but that would be operating the "zone of excellence." Lots of people are already doing this, and I would not be creating something unique, just presenting the same information differently. That's not at all satisfying to me.

I would agree with Hendricks' assertion, that for fulfillment you want to be in the "zone of genius." That has proven true for me!

Julene Ewert:

I work in both zones. First, working on a new idea and bringing it to life - my zone of excellence. Once my idea is alive and working well, I am in my zone of genius. But I find my fulfillment in both realms. I love to learn new things and push myself to come up with something completely different, which is fulfilling in itself. And to be known for this is the genius part. Bouncing back and forth feels right; it means that I am in a constant creative ebb and flow.

Erin Fickert-Rowland:

I have not had the opportunity to read this book yet, but I would agree that to feel fulfilled in our work, we need to reach the point where we have explored our passion so thoroughly that we extend beyond the ordinary and into the realm of "genius." Malcolm Gladwell's book, "Outliers: The Story of Success," provides many excellent examples of this happening for people who are outstanding examples of creativity and leadership in their field.

"Excellence" can be viewed as a trait that can be obtained along the way to "Genius," by always finishing work to our very best ability at that particular moment in time. It can also be a measure of public appreciation and acceptance. For example, a business would be performing at a level of "excellence" if it was seeing sales and profit. I think this has to be something a business owner strives for to feel fulfilled. Sometimes, working at the "Genius" level may be very personally fulfilling, but might be beyond the scope of an audience's appreciation. Failing to gain the support of a customer base can leave one feeling very isolated and unfulfilled. Therefore, I think there needs to be a balance. As creative business owners, we need to unceasingly explore and build new paths to offer customers fresh and exciting choices, but also realize that we need to be able to engage them through frequent open dialogues.

I am constantly searching and finding that balance in my business. I push myself and my materials to new levels of creativity, but then I find I need to back off to re-engage my customer base. When I am continually learning and growing, I feel personally fulfilled, but I don't know that I would tout that as "Genius!"

Louise Gale:

To me the zone of genius is letting those creative juices flow freely, taking different ideas and molding them together in such a way that you combine something new and exciting. I have a notebook of ideas I capture (or sometimes scraps of paper depending on where I am!), that I re-visit now and again for inspiration. It is also learning and growing when you are in that zone that sparks the creative genius.

Laura Gaffke:

I think my "genius" is when I am in what many would describe as "flow." It is when creating comes easy and I am lost in my work without judgment. It is when I TRUST my intuition and do not play victim to what everyone else is doing or has done. I feel free to experiment and make mistakes, knowing that this is where growth occurs and the magic happens.

Carrie Schmidt:

For me, working in the zone of genius means getting outside my comfort zone while painting and trying new things, exploring unknown territory. Sometimes I have a painting that looks fine, but I try to push myself to go for something more than just satisfactory.
  Taking risks, pushing your boundaries and stretching beyond your (perceived) limitations allow breakthroughs to occur—in art, business and life. I think doing this makes room for moments of genius to happen.

Valerie Hart:

Gay Hendricks says that in your Zone of Genius that work doesn't feel like work. I totally agree with this. I have experienced that feeling my entire life as a creative person. Throughout my advertising career, designing everything from logos to billboards — there were so many days when the time would just fly by. I still have this same experience in my art business whether I am painting or designing something on my Mac.

Elizabeth Gonzalez:

This is so true. When I try to concentrate on excellence I get lost and confused. When I work with the zone of genius I work confidently and I trust my instincts and my journey to what I want to accomplish. It is a combination of planning, intuition and enjoyment. I can feel it after the art piece is finished.

When I have a commission that involves only painting, I tend to procrastinate because I always look for the excellence zone first. After a few days struggling with the painting and my feelings I finally give permission to the zone of genius and everything starts to flow.

Amanda Fall:

I think the trouble sometimes is that our zones of excellence may be where we make money more easily. Genius might take you further into a niche. I do try to include both zones in Sprout, where most of the day-to-day actions are probably rooted in excellence. But when I try new things? When I expand, experiment, and blue-sky dream? Then the genius comes in.

E'Layne Koenigsberg:

The genius is what I'm talking about in an earlier question... getting in the "zone" to tap into the place of never ending creative energy. We can create from our heads and that is a zone of excellence but I believe when we create from the "zone of genius" we are definitely tapping into the realm where angels and gods and goddesses reside and share with us a window into the infinite.

Beth Doan:

I have not read the book, but I did research what it is about for this question. I am in the zone of excellence at my day job. I am fortunate to have a great day job that I like very much, while I grow my Art Business. I am on my way toward the zone of genius with my Art Business. I admit that I still do not take enough risks with my Art.

Liv Lane:

Ha! I actually interviewed Gay about this a while back {when I was still hosting a radio show}. I think that old adage is true: "time flies when you're having fun." There's a big misconception that if you're having fun, you must not be working hard. The key for me is to do work that feels so fun and meaningful that time just flies. Work doesn't have to be hard to make an impact or deliver abundance. There are lots of things I'm good at – that we're all good at – but that doesn't mean those things are good for us.

I work with women and youth on finding their spark – those innate passions that give our lives purpose and joy. When you hit it, you know it because it feeds you and it feeds others. That's where I'm at in my work now, which feels more like play. 2012 has been the first year in which everything I've made money doing was my own doing; I wasn't dependent on showing up for work somewhere or supplementing my income with freelance gigs I dreaded. I'm able to turn down those kinds of offers in order to do what I love – because being in that zone attracts enough income for me to do so. I'm incredibly grateful.

Mandy Saile:

This is a difficult one to answer, ha ha, especially without having read the book and getting the entire context of that statement/question. Hmmm…. I think for me, there are days when I make a picture or some whimsical goodie and I know it's 'safe' for me, I know it's something I can easily do, it's something I've done before. Maybe it's the 5th or 6th image in a series of birds for example and though I know I am enjoying the process of creation, I am in a way not pushing myself super hard. I think that may be when I am working in the zone of excellence.

But on those days where I push past the series work, where I dive into a new conceptual work which has hidden symbolism and this big long secret dialogue and story going on as I work on it, when I am not quite sure how it'll turn out and I push ahead anyways, when I hit those 'sticky' parts and feel like throwing the piece out but I make myself move forward anyways, I think that is the zone of genius, when I am pushing my creativity.

I think I really feel this when I am working on my very conceptual illustrations/images….not just when I am making a pretty picture of a beautiful bird or a joyful hopping rabbit, though they have their own wonderful place too.

YOUR TURN:

In the Book: The Big Leap" by Gay Hendricks, he distinguishes between two zones that we work within: the zone of excellence and the zone of genius. Hendricks says to find true fulfillment in your work, you need to work in your zone of genius. How do you respond to this assertion and how are you experiencing this within your business?

Question #23

Who do you admire for their ability to take risks in their business and thrive?

Your soul knows the geography of your destiny. Your soul alone has the map of your future; therefore you can trust this indirect, oblique side of yourself. If you do, it will take you where you need to go, but more important it will teach you a kindness of rhythm in your journey.

-
John O'Donohue

Tony Robbins

I had not really paid attention to him until about 6 months ago when I came across a YOUTUBE video featuring Robbins and Oprah Winfrey. I had a misconception about who he is and what his life's work is. His work revolves around helping people to see their circumstances as they are and then looking for ways to make it better.

This has been a prominent pattern in my life over the last decade. The discipline to come out of extreme financial straits one step at a time all the while hoping to God that we would not have to file bankruptcy has been the most challenging game plan of our lives. Hoping that my children would not be devastated by the uncertainty our family was living in. This is very similar to the type of background Tony Robbins started from.

Mr. Robbins is more than the hype you may have heard. And it has helped me to dig deeper into less of the fast money feeling that can be so alluring when you need to pay the bills. The slow and steady way…. More purpose, more meaning, more value…

Lisa Wilson:

I see many well-known figures, public figures, who seem successful in their business – and who have certainly taken their share of risks. But in admiring someone, I admire the person, not the accomplishments. I don't know what drives each of these people, who they've stepped on or helped along the way, what areas of their life they have sacrificed in order to thrive in the results I / we can see. So while I am impressed, I can't say I fully admire them.

On the other hand, I do know some personally who have taken risks and who I deeply admire. Just one example is Connie Hozvicka of Dirty Footprints Studio (http://www.dirtyfootprints-studio.com). In the summer of 2010, she quit her secure job as a teacher to make Dirty Footprints her full-time venture. Since then, she's created countless successful programs and allowed herself and her business to change and grow. Because of her flexibility, willingness to continue on through challenges, openness to all things dark and light, and trust in the overall process, she continues to thrive as a women, a business owner, and as a new mommy.

Catherine Just:

Sir Richard Branson (risk taker extraordinaire) , Danielle Laporte (wrote fire starter sessions out of necessity and created a sensation), Bono (rock star turned philanthropist), Gwen Stefani (was scared to death to be the lead singer, did it anyway, then did fashion too, and a family) , Marie Forleo (smart business woman, love her videos and how she hams it up to make a point), Laura Roeder (firing her clients and starting over and making it BIG), Brene Brown (telling the truth), Elizabeth Gilbert (writing something out of the ordinary for her turned into her biggest success), Madonna (master of re-invention and risk taking) , Robert Downey Jr (because he too had a similar experience that I had with drugs and alcohol and he rose up from the ashes to transform himself and his life and business).

Kat Sloma:

So many people! Kelly Rae Roberts was my first exposure to a creative business, through her Flying Lessons e-course in 2010. I like to watch how she shifts and adjusts her business to fit her life as she changes and grows.

Since taking that e-course, it's been fun to watch my "Fellow Flyers" from the class start to soar. One of my favorites to watch has been Beth Nicholls, who has created many wonderful ways to encourage others through her Do What You Love business. She's had to put herself out there and take risks, investing both money and time, to create her wonderful offerings, but it always seems to work out for her! I'm a huge fan of what she's created.

Nataša May:

My biggest inspiration at the moment is Tracy Verdugo. She had made such progress in this year alone I am in awe. She doubled her prices for her artwork which I think takes major guts in regards of not losing clients and she started teaching at art retreats all over the world. A true inspiration. :)

Julene Ewert:

I admire all women who are both chasing and creating their dreams. I admire Kelly Rae Roberts for "just going for it" and continuing to reinvent herself. I admire Cori Dantini for her dig-in approach and thriving in this economy and art climate - she has a good sense of humor too, which can't hurt. I admire Mati Rose McDonough for her spunk and colors. I also admire Kate Jaeckel for having a focus, high expectations, goals and incredible drive. All of these women are driven to succeed while having fun along the way. It's not easy for any of them, or us coming up the hill. But you can see that the risks they have taken have paid off.

Erin Fickert-Rowland:

I found this to be a hard question, because it is based on a lot of outside perception, and "thrive" is a subjective term. I consider inner happiness, a successful personal life, and quality of work to be big factors in my determination of "thriving." For example, I may see someone selling a lot of art, which displays little to no thoughtful execution or personal growth, and I don't consider that to be a success. On the other hand, I find countless examples of artists humbly achieving small milestones in their art and business, while balancing family and other obligations, and these are the people I greatly admire.

I admire women who have been working a long time with their medium (Painting, Jewelry, Collage, etc), and then figure out a way to step out onto their own unique platform. This allows them to expand their creative offerings beyond their art to teaching, writing and being consultants within their industry. I am thankful for these women providing wonderful business examples to other artists, like myself!

Laura Gaffke:

There are SO many people I admire for their risk taking gusto! Marisa Heidike of Creative Thursday is someone I have followed for some time. Her podcasts share her creative journey in such an upbeat, authentic way. I appreciate the way she notes the ups and downs of her creative business while always remaining positive and reflective. Her online classes and blog are insightful, rich and honest.

Jessica Swift is another person I admire. In her book "Jump Trust Repeat" she lets you into her creative journey and reminds you to trust you intuition, try new things and let go of what no longer serves you.

My husband Brett, although not in the creative business world, teaches me so much about what it takes to keep a business thriving. Watching him adapt to a changing economy in his line of business all the while staying positive when things are not necessarily positive around him makes me appreciate him even more.

Others I would like to note are Kelly Rae, Roberts, Flora Bowley, Alyson Stanfield, the ladies of the Teahouse Studio and my peers.

Juliette Crane:

Right now I really admire Marie Forleo, Danielle Laporte, and Kris Carr. Each is an inspiring entrepreneur and author who focus on how they can use what they know and love to help others.

I admire each for consistently taking a step back from their business and refining it and realigning it in a direction that works best for them. I've also heard each say that in planning the next 9-12 months of their business they've focused on the specific feeling they want to have more of in their life. In addition to coming up with new creative ideas and producing new products that help and inspire others, I love that these ladies take the time to take care of themselves and move forward with intention.

Amanda Fall:

Amanda Oaks, curator of Kind Over Matter (among other amazing new ventures), has been a major inspiration to me. She is always focused on clarifying her message, distilling and making it more powerful—leaving behind anything that isn't bold and beautiful. She innovates continually, while still prioritizing her family and her own self-care. Hoo-rah!

E'Layne Koenigsberg:

I had the pleasure of taking the class Hello Soul Hello Business with Kelly Rae Roberts and Beth Nicholls. They both have taken big risks in business which has paid off in a big way. I admire both of these women so very much...their ability to be vulnerable and their graciousness in sharing their knowledge so freely.

Beth Doan:

Kelly Rae Roberts. There are probably others, but she is the first person that pops into my head and I feel that the e-course I took a couple of years ago has had a huge impact on my believing that I can take my Business to the next level and eventually have it become the source of my full time income.

Liv Lane:

Erin Newkirk, who founded Red Stamp, has turned her online stationery store into a technology powerhouse; she built her business knowing that her passion was helping others stay connected in meaningful ways. As people sent snail mail less and less, she didn't let the downturn in stationery sales sink her business. Instead, she figured out ways to evolve it, serving customers in new ways while staying true to her purpose.

Red Stamp is now known for its iPhone app, which people use to send cute and colorful notes and photos to each other on their phones {with an option to print them out, too}. It's just genius.

Mandy Saile:

There are so many people to look up to. Almost every day I see a new artist and I think 'wow look at what they are doing' and I question 'how did they get that opportunity' and I think 'I bet I could do that too' and it's a constant game of not getting down but of reminding myself that these successful people are getting these chances because they are putting themselves out there and really applying themselves to the opportunities. They are going after what they want, simple as that.

Sure there are many of us who never seem to get the opportunities and chances dropped in our laps like others do, let's admit it, some artists have lucky horseshoes, magic leprechauns or just way more luck than the rest of us, ha ha, but I think it's key to remember that we're only in a race and competition with ourselves and that every artist has a different path.

We can't compare ourselves to others successes because we often don't see all of the cogs and wheels and decisions that took place to get them where they are. All we can do is make sure our paths and routes are as abundant with beauty and with trying as can be.

So, the list of artists that I admire is very long and the reasons I admire each are so varied…Off the top of my head I would have to mention Lori Portka, for the super kind, generous and beautifully spirited heart that she keeps throughout all of her business ventures. Kelly Rae Roberts is an inspiration for her just go for it attitude. Elsita Mora just for her continual spring of utterly beautiful diverse artwork whiles carrying on a beautifully busy life with children, etc. Genine Zlatkis for having such a strong style that so very naturally shines through whatever medium she touches. All of these lovely women seem so very humble and full of gratitude as well while never apologizing for the abundance in their lives, I love and admire that.

There are so many others, above all however I must confess that my main idols are the immensely inspiring, strong and beautiful: advocate and activist Jane Goodall, musician Peter Gabriel and Gloria Grow of the Fauna Foundation and also all the amazing souls out there who are strong enough and care enough to run and operate animal rescues like the Rabbit House Society or PETA or The World Wildlife Foundation, they all remind me of the beautiful human spirit I want to be in this life.

YOUR TURN:

Who do you admire for their ability to take risks in their business and thrive?

Question #24

Talk about a big risk that you took that had a positive result. What did you learn?

When I dare to be powerful, to use my strength in the service of my vision, then it becomes less and less important whether I am afraid.

-
Audre Lorde

Self publishing felt like such a daunting task for me. The formatting and the editing process in particular.

So with my first project I began to set it up as an e-course. And then slowly I began to realize what a commitment to would be to run an e-course.

But I figured out when I was about 80% through creating the material that I was going to use as information and assignments that I had essentially created the nuts and bolts of a book. From that exercise of moving forward in what I thought I would do, I actually set myself up to easily translate the information into an e-book.

What I learned:

- Begin

- Take little steps forward. The smallest step is bigger than you think.

-It is OK to change your course

Lisa Wilson: I have a challenging time thinking about risks and actions in terms of positive and negative results, because they are only positive or negative based on our limited view. How many times have we felt like a complete failure, only to look back at that time many years later and say, "thankfully THAT happened or I'd never be HERE!"

I see a risk as an action we take that has fear attached. The greater the fear, the greater the perceived risk. I've learned, as trite as it sounds, that taking risks is just another way to learn, to experience life. I've learned that trusted friends are far more valuable than money – honest friendship provides far more security than any amount of money. I've learned that the more we become comfortable with discomfort, the less there is to fear – and thus, the more risk we can take. Whether it's opening a new class, presenting a new work of art, or going for a longer run, the anxiety that arises becomes simply part of the experience, neither good nor bad, and certainly not an obstacle.

In my business, I experience a tiny bit of anxiety every time I hit "publish" on a blog post or "send" on a mass email. In many ways, "surviving" those small risks prepares me for the bigger ones…and allows me to become more engaged with the process instead of attached to the outcome. (Getting attached to even a positive outcome can create a harmful chain of desire.)

While there are a few bigger risks that have resulted in changes (strengthening) my business message, leaps in numbers of connections / followers, and public exposure, I think one of the most valuable risks to share is one that had more internal than external consequences.

Several months ago, out of the blue, I was contacted by Mark Lipinski, who runs a weekly, online radio show – Creative Mojo (http://toginet.com/shows/creativemojo). He was interested in having me as a guest on his show that Wednesday (only a few days away from the invitation).

I only became nervous when I researched who he was – among other things, an Emmy-Award nominated producer who has worked with the Oprah show – and about his show – with over 40,000 potential listeners. I was unbelievably nervous, and made the knowledge quite public (see my post about that here: http://lifeunity.com/blog/am-i-allowed-to-be-nervous.html.)

I spoke for maybe 20 minutes on air (did I mention this was LIVE)? And when it was done, I hung up the phone...and just sat there for a minute. Making a long, anxiety-ridden story very short, I didn't get any new followers from this. I didn't get a huge surge in traffic, or any calls from Oprah.

What DID shift was something inside. I'd just completed something in real time that terrified me. It hadn't gone as well as I'd hoped, but I hadn't cursed or burped. I was honest (even though my voice was shaking). And I survived.

I listened to the recorded podcast only once, and that was all it took to hear the uncertainty and nervousness in my voice. That was all it took to realize that I had absolutely no reason to be this afraid, and that, in staying caught in this fear, I would never be able to fully speak my truths.

In the 24 hours that followed, I was in an odd state – almost floating. I kept thinking, now what? Several deep breaths later, I kept right on going. I now held this odd sense of peace. It wasn't confidence, per se – I knew I'd still mess up here and there. It was just peace with how I was proceeding.

Since then, my site and my messages have had re-do's, and I've connected with many others – all in much stronger ways. It is a knowing now, unblocked by fear of that "BIG MOMENT" of what might happen. It already happened. I'm still here.

What can I share with you? Release expectations. They only get in the way. Try one big, terrifying thing. When it's over, you'll know, and you can move on with the more important things – like this moment. In running a business, speak your truths, kindly, and then continue on. It's what you are here to do – what we are all here to do.

Catherine Just:

Created the Soul*Full Summit and the Fear*Less Movement and interviewed people that I admired.

I learned that I love interviewing people, I learned that I am not afraid to ask for what I want, I learned that people resonated with what the topic was and that it continues to grow. I learned that being myself and putting myself out there without a mask of perfection - is the best road to take for me. I'm not afraid to be myself and be seen. I learned that I deeply want people to live the life of their dreams and I want to help support them in letting go of the fears that get in the way. I learned that this is part of my purpose. I learned that I am indeed a spiritual guide even though I personally don't love saying that.

Katie Clemons:

I think the bravest thing is putting your first item out into the world with a price tag. It's saying, "Hey! My creations are worth something," and that's a scary thing.

Kat Sloma:

For me, the biggest risk was moving from being a blogger to being a creative instructor online as I started my business. To make that transition happen I took risk personally, in my reputation and my ego, as well as the risk of the investment of my time and some money. There were so many questions: Could I make the transition and still maintain the core of who I am as an artist? Would people accept me as an instructor and be interested in my offerings? Would the investment of time and money pay off? The answer turned out to be yes to all. Maybe not immediately, but with continued time and energy, the risk has paid off.

Each risk I've taken, big or small, expands my comfort zone and gives me more room to operate without fear. When I take risk, I'm sometimes disappointed or perplexed by a result, but ultimately if I stay true to my heart I end up in a good place. There are times I've had to correct my course along the journey as things haven't worked out, but I don't see that as a failure. I see that as a fact of life. We always have to adjust as circumstances change.

Julene Ewert:

I ran my business for a few years on nights and weekends while working full-time and raising a baby. For one year I juggled everything. I trimmed my hours down at my "real" job, so I could work more at home. My goal: to leave my full-time job completely. After I quit my day job, which was a huge step, business boomed. It was a lot of hard work and long hours to make a similar salary. When you work for yourself, you wear every hat imaginable! I think you have to be a risk-taker to run your own business.

Erin Fickert-Rowland:

A big risk I took recently was taking several months off to really organize and set up an effective studio. This was a big investment of time and money- time that I didn't generate any new products to create income. I have learned that having an organized and efficient working space is indispensible. Not only is a beautiful studio presentable and welcoming to clients, but it is inviting and inspiring for my own time to work and create. Both of these are necessary to reach my long-term business and creative goals.

I have already had a very good response from my audience, and I have been pleasantly surprised at how much excitement about my business this milestone has generated for me. It has contributed to my professional credibility, not to mention my peace of mind.

Louise Gale:

To this day the best biggest risk I took that has had a positive result was believing in myself and leaving my corporate job to live a more creative life. Hands down. Everything has flowed from that decision and taken me on many different journeys, thought patterns and experiences. I have learned to listen to my intuition more as we do have the answer inside of ourselves and it has re-enforced my belief that everything really does happen for a reason.

Kim Gann:

I opened a shop. I had no support but I KNEW I could do it. I posted the hours and waited. Few customers came but some inquired about art lessons, so I created some classes. Took flyers to the local schools, had signs made and put them everywhere. The classes filled quickly. I taught there for 6 years. I still have my space and am preparing to begin classes again, after a 5 year break. I learned that a small shop has a hard time competing with the big guys, but the small shops can offer a service that the big guys can't

Cindy Silverstein:

I have been an artist for a very long time, doing freelance design work and illustration for many years before deciding that I would follow my dream of being a full time mixed media painter. I wanted to be completely in charge of my design decisions, my time and my direction as a creative person.

This journey has meant not only artistic freedom, which has been immensely satisfying; it has been a catalyst for personal growth more transforming than I had ever imagined possible.

In general, I am not what one might consider a risk taker by nature. Risk is scary. That's fine for brave folks, but not for me. I'm more the Woody Allen type. Many ordinary things seem scary to me. Putting myself out there, making contacts, meeting deadlines, taking care of all the unseen details of running a business can really scare me from time to time.

Enter e-course called Flying Lessons, with Kelly Rae Roberts. I had seen her work, I had her book, "Taking Flight," and I just wanted to learn everything she had to offer. I was extremely excited about taking a course with her and I registered right away. That was a big leap for me because I knew it meant I was committing myself to something greater than what I had aspired to in the past. I was going to go for it... a successful art career in the world of mixed media. I came out of the course with a great deal of valuable knowledge about things that would really grow my business.

So, craving more, I took Hello Soul Hello Business with Kelly Rae Roberts and Beth Nichols, which resulted in spiritually artistic development and greater business acumen. I think the most valuable lesson that came out of taking these first two courses was that I was creating this business and that I could create it in a form that would work with my own style and values.

Two more courses followed that have assisted me in getting to a place where I feel I have a much stronger foothold in the world of mixed media. Those two courses are Montage with Vivienne McMasters, about how to make soulful videos, and Build a Blog you Truly Love with Liv Lane. With the knowledge and resources I was given by these generous women, I had tools to work with to develop a business along with a growing internet presence so necessary for business in the arts today.

The big risk occurred for me when I realized I had to be brave enough to make the commitment to myself and my business and to keep that commitment alive. As a result of my effort, I have a cohesive style that runs throughout all my artwork and all the platforms of my online presence; I have a strong sense of passion, commitment and purpose in my artwork; and I am part of a huge community of like-minded artists and art aficionados who love and support one another with great enthusiasm. This took time, practice, patience, and a belief in the possible even when things seemed impossible.

Laura Gaffke:

The biggest risk I have taken to date was leaving my tenured teaching position that I loved and going to graduate school to earn my Masters in Fine Arts. I had been teaching art for almost 14 years but had always had an inner "knowing" or "soul calling" that I was meant to grow my art in a way that teaching full time would not allow for. Leaving this job was the hardest thing I have ever done as it had brought so much joy to my life, shaped who I had become and really was part of my identity.

It turned out that taking this risk was the greatest gift of my life. It was where I had the time and space to truly explore my art, ask deep questions and define what was important to me. Goddard College, with its progressive educational philosophy, was where I found my voice as an artist. I went from painting very traditional landscape paintings to exploring and researching ideas about friendship, spirituality, and ecology, all of which inform my work today. Becoming clear about the intentions behind my work and what is really at the heart of it has given me the confidence to take myself seriously as an artist and share my work with the world.

Juliette Crane:

A year into my business I launched my first online course, HOW TO PAINT AN OWL. I had no idea what I was doing, but I was lucky enough to have an incredible support group for guidance and had taken some amazing online courses that had really moved me and made me know just what I wanted to share in my own class.

At the same time I was starting from scratch- I didn't know how to structure the course, how to record videos, or what platform to use, let alone how I would get people to sign up for my class. But putting myself out there and following my intuition to create my first online course was the best thing ever. It taught me so much about myself and gave my business a real purpose that continues to propel me forward.

Since then, I've developed two additional courses (HOW TO PAINT A GIRL and HOW TO CREATE WHIMSICAL ANIMALS). That first course gave me a place to begin. I try and remember that whenever I launch a new creative project. It's always a starting point, knowing it will evolve from there. It doesn't have to be perfect. The most important part is to get started and put whatever it is I need to get out there. From there, the resources and audience falls into place because, for me, once I'm started I know what I need to grow and can seek it out. But at first, any project is always a big idea and it usually evolves in some way. But I can't get to that evolution unless I take those first steps.

Now teaching has really reshaped my business and given rise to purpose in my life...something I never realized I could have or was even searching for. But I am so glad I followed those initial instincts and took a big risk.

Elizabeth Gonzalez:

I quit my professional job with no safety net of having the money to make a living. After that day I was more focused and I started to take my artist "job" or creative business seriously. It has been hard but delightful. Every single day I am sure that I am where I want to be and doing what I want to do. Any difficult situation has a lesson in it and we become stronger and confident. Those "not so good days" always have something positive and I try hard to focus on that, the things that made the day a gift. When something goes wrong I say this to myself:

Stop worrying
Breathe
Think
Do something that makes you happy
Think of all your blessings
Tomorrow is another day and a new beginning
Count your achievements
You are strong
Have faith and hope for the best

And in a matter of a few minutes (OK sometimes hours!) I feel relieved and at peace.

Mary Nasser:

A big risk that I took was beginning my blog two years ago. I am a quiet, private person, so starting a blog felt very scary! But being a quiet person is exactly what made it critical for me to begin my blog– to let people see my process and inspiration and connect to me as an individual.

Keeping a blog has had profound results for me! I've connected with others and become a part of a larger artistic community; I've been fortunate enough to communicate with many other creative people all over the world through blogging. Blogging has helped me create goals for both my blog and my life, and attain goals. Keeping a blog keeps me accountable.

Also, I've created more art than ever since beginning my blog. I research with purpose and have a sense of consistency and grounding – with the ups and downs of life, blogging remains a constant in mine. Blogging has helped me accomplish more than I ever thought I could! Recently, I learned that 4 of my mixed-media map paintings have been published in issue #2 of Featuring Magazine – including one of my paintings on the front cover! I couldn't be more thrilled! It's been a dream of mine to have my paintings featured in a print magazine! And Featuring Magazine is an international magazine with the publisher based in the Netherlands and an international team!

Amanda Fall:

Committing wholeheartedly to this Sprout journey is one of the biggest professional and heart-and-soul risks I've ever taken. To do it right, I've had to pour in countless hours and devote huge amounts of energy and dedication—all without any guarantee that anyone would like it or buy it (and considering that I work full-time at Sprout, I need that cash flow to be sustainable).

Every day I pinch myself and say a prayer of gratitude for where I am now, what feels like a world away from that early-on doubt and fear and debilitating worry. I have come to trust my instincts, to believe that my dream is more than worth my effort, and that what I have to give is needed by the world. And to trust that people DO love Sprout—almost as much as I do!

E'Layne Koenigsberg:

While visiting Cedar Key, Florida, I saw a beautiful waterfront store on stilts for rent. I called a dear artist friend and asked if she wanted to open an art gallery with me...even though the town was 2 ½ hours from our city. In a split second she said yes and Wild Woman Gallery was born. It grew into four galleries in several regions of Florida. We were very successful and had lots of fun.

Being reflective now I did learn you can spread yourself too thin. In business you have to wear every hat even with business partners and that can be really time consuming.

Katherine Quinn:

A big risk {big as in emotional rather than financial} I took was to approach a fellow artist and business owner I admire about working on a project together... It was my first potential collaboration and I was really nervous about being rejected.

So my plan was to ease into the conversation to get a feel of how things sat with her before I put any suggestions her way. It was funny... after talking about the kids etc... I asked how things were going with her business and she talked about how she needed something different to focus on and was thinking of asking some artists to do some designs for her and was thinking of approaching me!!!

Beth Doan:

My first reaction to this question was, I don't believe I've taken any big risks yet, but then I looked at the question from another angle and emotionally, I took a big risk, when I opened up my online Etsy shop and created separate bank accounts for it. It was a big deal to me. It was the first time I actually took myself seriously as an Artist and put myself out there for the world to see who I am. I learned that I am capable to run a business and that any fear that I would lose the joy of my Art by making it a business was unfounded and not true. My desire, love and need to create have actually increased ten fold.

My next big risk will be to expand my offerings and run my Art Business full time.

Mandy Saile:

I think quitting my job as a gallery coordinator was huge leap for me. I loved the job but it was a very full and busy one that left me with little energy after work (as is the usual story I suppose) it was a job that I was lucky to have, especially given the small city I lived, a lot of young people clamored after the position I was in, but the pay was horrible and after a time I started getting so tired of hanging other artists' work and making it look good.

I wanted to do that for myself too. And I knew I needed to move forward with my work and my style but a full time job wasn't allowing me to take that step forward, so after a lot of deliberation, and with immensely beautiful support from my sweetheart, I resigned to pursue my own artwork full time. Though my business is not where I feel it should be and though I feel like I have a really long way to go, waking up every morning, knowing I can concentrate on my artwork, my business, my honey, my bunnies and manage my migraines a lot easier from the comfort of my own home/studio, feels like such a huge huge blessing...so yes, I think leaving that job, was a giant step into the beloved life I currently have.

Also, when I was fresh out of college and so afraid of everything still, I mustered up the courage to submit my illustration portfolio to an environmental magazine and they hired me, my very first illustration job, for the front glossy cover of the magazine. That was a purely exciting and pleasant illustration assignment and experience.

YOUR TURN:

Talk about a big risk that you took that had a positive result. What did you learn?

Question #25

Talk about a big risk that you took that had a negative result. What did you learn?

Hold fast to your dreams, for without them life is a broken winged bird that cannot fly.

Langston Hughes

I have a strong opinion about taking on other people's big projects. I will not do it. At first, you might look at it as a great opportunity. But beware. Because you never know all the details. All the traps. All the politics. The reality of why the person is walking away from the project.

And then... you are left with the turmoil, the headache, the need to explain things that you do not understand. The buck is passed to you and guess what? You do not know what caused the bill that has come due.

It is never worth it in my opinion. You might as well toil with your OWN vision. Take on the headaches because you believe in the outcome. Stay in it longer because you are ready for the backlash, the complications, the failures that may come.

And guess what? When you see the project from beginning to end, it is TRULY YOUR PROJECT. No excuses. No shared success. It is authentically and beautifully YOU that is allowed to shine.

Lisa Wilson:

As I mentioned in an earlier question, I've taken risks that had an immediate negative result – but none that have not been beneficial in one way or another. In fact, I had a hard time coming up with a specific response for this question. Each time I thought of a risk (some fear-laden action), I would consider how thankful I am that it happened, regardless of the immediate outcome.

It's taken many years to get LifeUnity to where it is now. In fact, it has actually evolved from a coaching business to a general wellness business to a photography business to what it is now. And through those changes, I've "failed" at several attempts….many with large financial outlays.

(I share an example only because many of us like the "fail" stories. It helps us know that we are not alone, that it is OK to go through these things!)

Back when coaching was just beginning as a career path, I was deeply immersed in learning all about it. I attended online and in-person trainings, shelling out hundreds of dollars that we (as a young married couple just out of college) didn't really have to spend. By the time I had business cards, a website, and happy clients through my coaching business, I had already been through many of the fears and resistance. I was starting to come out on the other, "successful" side.

But something remained...a nagging voice that wouldn't stop. It kept telling me that this wasn't my path. It came out in dreading coaching calls and lethargy when trying to design more around my business. But I resisted – after all, I'd already put in all of this investment!

Needless to say, I quit coaching not long after that. It seemed as though all of the money and time spent had been a waste. Remember, though, that was only through an immediate perspective. I learned a tremendous amount, and am so glad that I "failed" at that path. I learned that you have to be constantly mindful when going on a path – any path in life - and, if it isn't working, to change paths. (There's a difference between pursuing despite discomfort, giving up, and ignoring wise intuition. You learn the difference through mindful practice.)

I learned that you can't be afraid to fail; otherwise, you'll spend your entire life trapped in a path where you aren't outwardly failing, but inwardly dying. I learned that negative results are negative only if you stop flowing with them. Results are results – consequences of actions. If we get caught in trying to interpret them instead of integrating them, we hold ourselves back.

Catherine Just:

I don't believe there is such thing as a negative result. It's all a big learning process. If something doesn't feel right I get to change my mind. If people don't like something I do and it doesn't work for them or for me, I can adjust it. It's all just information gathering. It's research. You can't learn unless you take action. I've learned a lot from taking action, seeing what works and what doesn't and adjusting or tweaking things until it really feels right and true for me. Everything I've done up to this point right now - is important. It all leads me to this moment right now.

Kat Sloma:

Ironically, the same big risk of starting my business had a negative impact too. I took on too much at the beginning — moving internationally from Italy back to the US, starting my business offering online classes within a few weeks of the move, and then offering a brand new class within a couple of months that I needed to create. A few months later I also transitioned to a new website. All of this was done while working 30-40 hours a week at my corporate job and having a family at home. It was way, way too much. I ended up with a month of stress headaches and shoulder pain from being on the computer excessively. My family was grumpy with me for not paying attention to them.

From this experience, I realized that I could overwhelm myself in my enthusiasm and turn my dreams into nightmares if I wasn't careful. I learned that I need to maintain a careful balance between all of the things I want to do and accomplish in my life. I am more careful in my planning and what I commit to now. Before starting something new, I ask myself: Does this activity resonate with my heart? Does it get me to where I want to go with my art and my business? Does it feed me in some way? What else will I have to give up in order to add this new thing? I pay careful attention to my heart as I answer these questions. If my heart is aligned, I can usually take on something new effortlessly, but I set limits now too.

Julene Ewert:

I developed a product that I was making myself. The product was featured in magazines and selling very well. To keep up with demand, I decided to have the product created in China. It was a wonderful learning experience to be involved in product development at that scale. I had to order a huge amount of inventory, and the product sold well for a few years. Then sales fell. I now have a sizable inventory of product that doesn't move quickly.

At first this made me feel terrible. I felt successful women don't make such mistakes. I've come to accept that sometimes they do, and really that is how success is made. We fall and then get back up. I learned that products and businesses have a cycle. Products sell well and then they cycle down. The trick is to know when this is happening. I've learned to start small and be very cautious about expanding. You never know what the future will throw at you.

Erin Fickert-Rowland:

The biggest risk I took didn't even feel like a risk- it felt like I was doing the right thing. I didn't realize the risk I was taking by over-extending myself with work and neglecting my health. This year I undertook a project that was too big, and coincided with too many extraneous obligations. It all seemed doable, until my neck clenched and locked up. I was in excruciating pain, and immediately unable to work. I was in rehabilitation for months.

During that time, I began to eat poorly, gain weight, and feel miserable. To keep myself motivated, I began to reevaluate what work was truly important to me, and what could be let go. I developed a plan to get back to work- even if it was only slowly at first. I worked with my doctors, diligently followed my rehab instructions, and got myself creating art again. I have been steadily gaining momentum ever since, and now I feel like I am stronger than I was before.

I learned that I can't do it all. I learned to set limits on my work. I learned to take my diet and exercise seriously. I learned that all of these things contribute to overall well-being, which makes me a better artist, a better business owner, and a better person.

Louise Gale:

Last year I made a mistake of not giving myself enough time to finish a new product I had already announced was coming out. Then something happened in my personal life which pushed me back further. It was a tough decision to make, but I had to cancel the course and refund money. I felt like it had a negative result as it went against one of my values of doing something I said I would do.

My main learning from this, was that it was okay to cancel it, rather than put something out into the world I wasn't happy with. It wasn't all negative of course, as I then ended up creating The "Creative Color Cleanse Program" { http://louisegale.com/shop/meditations-and-kits/color-bliss-mini-retreat-downloadable-kit/ } which is a full downloadable product that I love even more than the original course I designed, so as always I am glad I listened to my intuition.

Kim Gann:

I took a risk on a trade show. It was very costly. I 'thought' it was a place to be 'found' for art licensing. Afterwards I learned that, although I did my homework and I looked like a seasoned pro, I was still just a newbie without the information I needed. I learned that the websites and blogs that discuss and 'teach' about trade shows may not give all the information you need. You need to thoroughly check out endeavors before jumping in. If I had 'walked' the show first I would have known how the show worked and that contacts and appointments should be made ahead of schedule. Visit your competition. See what is and isn't working.

Juliette Crane: I never see anything, really, as a negative result. If I don't get the result I am hoping for, the situation most often provides a new perspective and bumps me in a new direction I wasn't planning on moving.

This was one of those pushed in a new direction moments for me: I had really been wanting to sign on with a licensing agent. I thought that was the next best move for me. And my ideal art agent was taking part in a pitch slam at a conference. It was one of those moments where I felt I had to go...this was my chance. I put together a portfolio, memorized my pitch and drove oh-so nervously to the conference. The pitch went as best as it could, but I didn't get that, "I want you, sign here," moment I'd been dreaming of. I felt I didn't get much of anything positive from the experience. I left the conference feeling completely deflated, like I didn't fit at all and I had really done my best.

Two weeks later I was asked to be part of the audience for Oprah's new show Life Class (with guest Eckhart Tolle). Crazy enough, I won the tickets because I'd answered a question on her website about seeming to have it all with my art business and still not feeling happy. That show changed my life.

Attending the taping moved me in a new direction as a result of my "negative" experience. I realized then that my heart was completely aching. But not because I didn't get something I wanted from the conference. My heart ached because something bigger was missing in my life and business. I realized licensing wasn't the best direction for me at that time. That I needed to follow my heart. And my heart was into writing, storytelling and creative projects that came directly from me, not based on what a licensing agent could do. My heart also sparked when I connected directly with people. I needed that connection to feel alive.

From that moment on, I changed the direction of my business from product-based longing and intense-forward-driven to ways that I could transform my passion into serving others and being in the moment. And that has changed my life.

With each new creative project I choose to work on now, I make sure I have that huge spark that lights me up inside and propels me to move forward. I need to be really excited about the project and it needs to be something that I'm not only passionate about, but that allows me to help others live their dreams and be their happiest.

Elizabeth Gonzalez:

In 2003 I asked for a no salary leave from my work as college professor and opened a "manufacturing" ceramic workshop. I created a partnership with a friend and my sister and everything went wrong. We hired 10 employees in less than a week with not enough cash flow, not all the employees were good, the business stuff was too much for me and I ended up with anxiety problems and prescribed drugs for anxiety and minor depression. I closed it after the first year and I am still paying debts from that business. I learned to trust my instincts and not follow advice from people that don't know anything about what you want. I learned that it was not the kind of business I was dreaming of.

Amanda Fall:

Honestly, I'm not sure that any risks I've taken have been truly negative. When I look back over my journey as a creative (writer, artist, etc.), I've certainly been on a long and winding path since graduating college as an art major. I tried so many things that flopped or were only minimally successful or ended up costing more soul than I got back. I made stationery (loved it, but didn't make enough profit), sold at craft shows (ohhh, man, that is a TOUGH business!), set up an Etsy boutique (exciting but couldn't get enough traction)—all of these could technically be labeled risks that had negative results.

But guess what? Each had so many positives. Each led me closer to where I am now. I made contacts and widened my network. I learned how to treat customers with respect and kindness. I figured out what I could spend all day doing without feeling worn to a nub (and, conversely, what DID wear me down). Looking back, I am so grateful for each of those attempts and can see how they helped me get where I am today.

E'Layne Koenigsberg:

Decades ago my then husband and I opened a restaurant...The Out of the Way Café and Boutique. The concept and business didn't make it. What did I learn...when people say retail business is all about location, location, location...they mean it!!! I also found out a lot about myself...I wanted to "create" a business...make up a menu, decorate the café, make products for the boutique, make a huge sign, name the business...what I didn't want to do was the everyday details of running a restaurant. I learned to think things through to the end result...what will my life look like on a day to day basis... and not get so caught up in the "idea" of a business.

Beth Doan:

I thought that to be a good mother and wife, I needed to put my desire to pursue my Art on the back burner. I thought that I couldn't do both well. I loved being a mother and raising my children, they were the best years of my life, but I did lose myself along the way. Ultimately, I ended up in a divorce a couple of years ago.

I have learned that I had the ability to do both, but didn't feel worthy or could not risk being anything but completely dedicated to my children and husband. And while I do believe I was a good mother and wife, I could have been an even greater mother in their growing years, if I had shown them by personal example that you can follow your dreams and still be a dedicate, involved, loving parent.

Looking back, I couldn't take the risk of trying to do both. I'll never know for sure, but I'm not sure my marriage would have survived, if I had asserted my needs and desires for my Artistic dreams. It was fine as a hobby, but not encouraged. What I got was, be careful, don't risk losing the joy of creating by making it a business obligation, if you turn your Art into a business, you will loose the joy of it.

So, with little self esteem and the desire to please, I believed this and wasn't willing to take any risks. I did not want my children to experience a broken home like I had growing up. It was not a bad life, but it could have been so much more. So, that just means that I have delayed my success and personal satisfaction of creating and sharing my Art with the world. I now have a new life, a new husband, who is my friend first, who truly understands, supports and encourages my dreams.

Mandy Saile:

Well there was an illustration job a few years back, illustrations for a book. I was told that it would be a fairly small job and only needing this and that. So to get the job I quoted a fairly low price and I got the job only to find that the work load was 3 times what I was originally told, there were a lot of changes and requests for my style to change which I did of course but which wasn't easy. It just all felt very unsatisfying, I felt under-paid and the biggest mistake I made was giving it 100% priority over all other opportunities. It was the sole thing I worked on for several months and in the end it didn't get published in the format it was supposed to and even though every illustration was approved and signed off on before I proceeded with the next, half of my work was replaced with soulless work of another artist with no explanation as to why. That was my worst experience thus far.

Also, recently I had a solo exhibition that had quite a few negative moments as well. There was a big mistake with the scheduling, I was booked in for a full month and the director gave 2 of my weeks away to another show without consulting me or even telling me at first! I had just a few hours to hang my entire show before the opening, and ended up too exhausted to enjoy my own opening. I was asked to take my show down early even! And I was promised help where it never came through. My invitations were messed up and embarrassing, and it was just one negative thing after the next it seemed...it soured me on galleries for awhile, but I am over it now, and realize I was as professional as I could be and that's all that I could have done...the lesson and test was to find positivity despite all of the negative and I feel like I did eventually manage to do that.

YOUR TURN:

Talk about a big risk that you took that had a negative result. What did you learn?

Question #26

What role has collaboration played in the success of your business? Describe one of your earliest collaborations and the results you experienced.

Each of us has an inner dream that we can unfold if we will just have the courage to admit what it is. And the faith to trust our own admission. The admitting is often very difficult.

Julia Cameron

The very first collaboration was with four other creative entrepreneurs: Sonya McCllough, Laura Otero, Kelly Thiel, Alease McClenningham. Sonya devised a project to work through the book "The Creative Entrepreneur" by Lisa Sonora Beam in 24 hours.

It was an insane amount of work and at the time I was in the process of transitioning back to the United States from Germany. What I learned is how incredibly dedicated each of my colleagues is to her business and to the passion which she offers to the world.

I have kept my eyes open for solid collaborations like this ever since.

Lisa Wilson:

I am always collaborating, whether explicitly or not. No business is ever built alone. From the financial support of my husband, the feedback of strangers on my blog, to the specific support from a few loved friends, we are all working together to make this happen.

This is why I am constantly and honestly saying 'thank you '. Every Facebook comment, shared insight, smile, hug, phone call or email is another opportunity for me to experience the beauty of sharing awareness.
Because many might be looking for something more specific, allow me to share a few collaborations that have been most helpful in getting LifeUnity to where it is now.

Very early collaborations took the form of emails bounced back and forth with friends or a late night chat over wine with my husband or siblings discussing logistics of LifeUnity.

Later collaborations took many forms. Those collaborations that were built on honesty, kindness, commitment, and flexibility are the ones from which I benefitted and which still remain in place today. For example, a weekly Skype date with a good friend and fellow entrepreneur has been ongoing for nearly two years now. Random calls with another inspirational and wise friend keep me informed and deeply motivated. More recently, I was honored to be invited to a Wisdom Council of approximately 10 women that meets virtually every two weeks. The connection into the Wisdom Council emerged from a very early online friendship that grew out of that premise of honesty and kindness.

Kat Sloma:

I've been involved in several different collaborations, and they can be great for your business. By working with others, you can generate some wonderfully creative ideas, as you build off of each other. You can also grow your respective audience, as you tap into the network each of the collaborators has.

One of my earliest collaborations was "Super Hero Summer Camp," a 6-week e-course delivered via email, created by six of us. It was five life coaches, each with a different coaching perspective (such as health, time management, finding your passion, etc.) and me, providing the creativity perspective. We each provided a week of content, worked together on the advertising, and promoted the event individually. It turned out to be a great success! I received many referrals from completely new sources, and got to know some wonderful women through the process of collaborating on the project.

Julene Ewert:

I have a small group of wonderfully creative friends who meet once a year to collaborate on artistic goals. The results are inspiring and uplifting. Both relaxing and invigorating! We keep in touch all year long to see where each of us is in our creative goals. We push, we love, we comfort and we are there for each other. It means the world to me to have this creative collaboration; I am not sure how I would make it through the challenging times without them.

Jodi Lebrun:

My first collaboration came very unexpectedly and it blew my socks off! Back in Dec. of 2011 I was looking for a way to say thank you to the many women that I'd connected with, and some of whom had become my Mentors, over the course of 2011. I love to blog so I came up with the idea of writing a series of posts to publicly thank these women. I then had this flash that I should somehow include some of the talented ladies (including Robin Norgren, thank you!) that I'd met in the many e-courses that I'd taken or that I'd met online. I sent out a choppy email asking if anyone, despite it being the busy Christmas season, would be interested in submitting a guest post about what they are passionate about and thankful for.

Well, much to my surprise, the replies started to flood in with a resounding 'Yes!' and the next thing I knew I had a week of giveaways and guest posts! Readers were leaving comments from all over the world and it was the most magical feeling - getting to share these talented ladies with the world - I knew that I needed more of this. It was dubbed Art Share-a-Palooza 2011 and later turned into my first e-book (which you can get for free at www.creativelifebydesign.com). Fast forward a few months, with a new coaching certification and a renewed sense of confidence, I was able to launch Where The Spirited Women Gather, a blog dedicated completely to sharing the words and passions of my fellow creative and spirited women.

Erin Fickert-Rowland:

Collaboration has played a big role in the success of my business, which may be surprising, because I work by myself! However, here are three key examples of collaborations that have done wonders for my business:

> 1. **Approaching artists I admire to do feature stories on my blog.** This was actually one of the very first things

I started to do when I began blogging, and it taught me so much. I love learning about other artists and their creative process. Interviewing them contributes to building wonderful relationships that are very rewarding, and challenges my writing skills. These collaborations helped me add wonderful articles to my blog, and also allowed me to help other artists with their marketing!

2. **Hiring a consultant to help me with my blog design.** This was invaluable! Not only did I learn an incredible amount of technical skills needed to develop and code my website, but we also built a wonderful friendship and working relationship.

3. Co-Hosting a Jewelry Donation and Blog Hop for The Global Genes Project. A friend and I started out as two people who wanted to donate a handmade bracelet to support the 7000 Bracelets for Hope Campaign. When we decided to combine our efforts and publicize it to our audiences, we gathered over 50 participants and were able to donate many more bracelets to support mothers with children that have extremely rare diseases. We were also able develop relationships with Global Genes, and help raise awareness about this organization, encouraging others to donate more bracelets and host their own hops!

Louise Gale:

I would really like to find more opportunities to collaborate. I love to work with others that have a shared vision where we all bring something exciting and great to the table. One of my earliest collaborations was for my online class "Big Dreams Small Wonders" { http://bigdreamssmallwonders.com/ } where I invited another life coach to host some of the lessons and also an energy kinesiologist to create some energy balancing exercises.

This class was first launched in January 2011 as an e-course and now has a workbook & planner product available { http://louisegale.com/shop/e-books/big-dreams-small-wonders-journal-planner/ } and also the full masterclass program { http://louisegale.com/shop/meditations-and-kits/big-dreams-small-wonders-master-class-program-download/ } as a downloadable product.

Laura Gaffke:

Collaboration is at the core of my business and a sacred part of who I am. It is what keeps me moving forward, holds me accountable and challenges me in ways I would never have stretched myself otherwise. One of my earliest and ongoing collaborations is with my friend and now business partner, Tina Hirsig. We met in grad school and started sending postcards to each other with the simple intention of "what could be learned through friendship and art." This morphed into a series of 6 x 6 inch art squares that we mailed to each other for over two years. These little gems allowed us to explore questions within our art, experiment with new techniques and share thoughts and ideas about what we were learning in both a visual and written form.

We have gone on to investigate topics such as "place", worked on a detailed collaborative book that took us over a year to take form, and continue to work on a bi-weekly project called Vision/Revision, which starts off with each of us posting an image on our blog "lauraTWOtina" on Mondays and "Revising" the image with a handmade piece of art that we send to each other and additionally are shared on our blog.

Our work together has led us to several shows of our work, a feature article in Artful Blogging magazine, a guest on Cassie Preemo Steele's "Co-Creating" Show and our first solo show coming up in March 2013 where we are working on a series called TAOS "Two Artists One Surface" that we are really excited about! All of these collaborative projects have helped me in my business by stretching me in ways that I would not have otherwise.

*You can learn more about these projects as well as other collaborative work on our blog, http://www.lauraTWOtina.com

Elizabeth Gonzalez:

My most recent experience with collaboration was for the Online Course Project. Without this collaboration the project would be impossible. I asked for collaboration in setting the Constant Contact marketing tool, the template for the webpage and the videos. The results were amazing because I could concentrate on the course content and the social media marketing. The main positive result is that I don't feel overwhelmed, making the experience smoother and enjoyable.

Amanda Fall:

Collaboration is a huge part of Sprout. Although I'm a solopreneur and all the day-to-day work of Sprout is done by me (layout, design, editing, networking, marketing, proofing, etc.), I love the interplay between guest contributors and myself. I get to bounce off their energy, finding pieces of my own that complement theirs (poetry, artwork, essays, and more). It's an exciting and ever-surprising way to work.

One of my most life-changing collaborations early on was with a dear friend, Natasha Reilly, of Creative Nachos. In May of 2010 we co-created and co-hosted an e-course called The Creative Playground. Wow, what an experience! It was amazing to have someone closely matched to share ideas with, to be honest with each other in what we thought needed to be tweaked, to encourage and lift each other when we struggled. Sometimes this business of creation can feel so lonely. Working with Natasha made me feel doubly strong.

E'Layne Koenigsberg:

I have had several collaborations...some successful...some not. I talked about my collaboration in Wild Women Gallery and that was successful because the two sisters I was in business were like family. We know our personal relationship and commitment to enduring friendship was paramount. With that vision we knew we could work out whatever business challenges came our way.

I learned it's important to have business partners that believe what you believe. If you are a very trusting person and operate from intuition and you partner with a person who is fearful and over thinks everything it wouldn't be a successful partnership.

Katherine Quinn:

I have only participated in one real collaboration and it is just in the beginning stages so there is no real success yet. Although in saying that, just making the contact has given me a huge boost and makes the thought of approaching someone else in the future easier.

Mandy Saile:

I haven't had any collaborations except for the recently new one I have selling a small series of my illustrations on these really cool interchange-able magnetic lockets with Cat Ivins of Polarity on Etsy. I had been following her work for some time just because she was one of the very successful sellers on Etsy and I had heard of her cool products time and time again and I saw that she was collaborating with several other artists I admired immensely, so I plucked up the courage to approach her and ask if she'd like to team up with me too and her response was so very positive and encouraging that though we're not selling large numbers (not yet anyhow!), I still deem it a successful venture and a great pairing up.

I've been approached by a few fellow Etsy sellers otherwise but I haven't entered into any collaborations because what they were selling was too similar to something I currently was already selling or have future plans to introduce in my own shop. I am always happy to consider new partnerships though and I am hopeful that some new perfect ones will come up soon.

YOUR TURN:

What role has collaboration played in the success of your business? Describe one of your earliest collaborations and the results you experienced.

Question #27

Do you have a formula for setting goals? How do you stay on track for achieving your goal?

Pick the day. Enjoy it – to the hilt. The day as it comes. People as they come... The past, I think, has helped me appreciate the present – and I don't want to spoil any of it by fretting about the future.

-

Audrey Hepburn

I mentioned that I have a morning quiet time. This is where the goals are birthed. I am amazed at how once I get really conscientious about letting the purpose of my business evolve that projects 'appear' in my mind's eye that initially seemed so insurmountable and then suddenly the time energy, the structure are suddenly in my heart to move forward.

Examples (my three workbooks/journals that I have self published):
30 Day Linger Journal: http://choosetolinger.blogspot.com/
Inspire Me with the Psalms:
http://www.inspiremewiththepsalms.blogspot.com/
Find Your Creative Voice:
http://findyourcreativevoice.blogspot.com/

And this book you have in your hands which began in 2012. The key is staying on track for me is to make sure you have solitude to help the growth in the early seedlings of a project and help you to maintain clarity and shed competing goals.

Lisa Wilson:

Perhaps surprisingly, no! No formulas. I've found that in getting attached to goals, I become more interested in the goal than in the process. When that happens, I find myself losing that sense of wonder described in an earlier question. Every step then becomes a tedious chore just to reach the goal...no matter how desirable the goal started or remains.

I stay on track by practicing mindfulness. When I am fully present, whether that's with my discomfort after being in front of the computer screen for two hours or in bliss while painting with my beeswax, I am always able to recognize what I need in that moment.

I set aside specific times where I am mindfully planning – that is, present with the process of setting goals or adding things to the calendar.

If I want to make sure I accomplish something by a specific date, I publically announce the date and the goal. Being accountable to others almost always ensures I will do what I promised. Otherwise, it is mindful step by mindful step, letting my intuition guide me, discomfort inform me, and the sense of wonder and exploration I have keep me motivated and disciplined.

Catherine Just:

I write out the end goals, and then I reverse engineer. I write out all the steps I need to take to get there. I have a wall calendar that shows the entire year at once, and I plan out everything and put it on the schedule. I allow for things to shift as I learn and grow. I give myself permission to change my goals.

I've built a supportive tribe around me to check in with. They tell me the truth if I'm not seeing something that could be re-directed. I see and feel the end goal as if it's already done. I really feel it in my entire being. It's already done, and I practice staying open to collaborating with the universe and the people who are brought into my life that partner with me to bring these goals into reality.

Kat Sloma:

I used to love this quote, "A goal without a deadline is just a dream." I see goals as specific and time-based. I've always been a goal-setter, and it's taken me far in life.

I like to plan, but I don't set a lot of concrete goals for myself in my creative business. It goes back to my ability to overwhelm myself. I'm a Type-A, overachiever personality so if I set a goal, I'm going to give everything to get there and will be terribly disappointed if I don't. I've discovered I enjoy myself more with by keeping an "idea list" instead of goals, which gives me the flexibility to shift my plans when the timing is right. I do work to deadlines and schedules, such as when I offer a new class or send my newsletter twice a month, but I also give myself options. While I have a yearly plan that outlines my planned class schedule, I don't publicize class dates too far in advance because things come up and I might want to change the schedule.

I keep a list of general ideas and then work on them when the time is right. For example, a couple of years ago I knew I wanted to start an email newsletter. I didn't set a specific timeframe for accomplishing this; it just hung out on my list of things to do. Six or eight months after I started to thinking about creating a newsletter, I had a specific project idea, the [Liberate Your Art Postcard Swap](), which seemed perfect for an email list. I knew I could use this project to help me learn how to use the email delivery service for my newsletter and delivery of my classes too, so I finally figured out how to set it up. The timing was right and it went smoothly.

I think it's important to realize when you are starting out; you can't do it all at once. When I look at people I admire in business, I often see all that they do and have established and feel like I should be there too. But setting up a solid business foundation can't happen overnight. I've learned to let myself grow organically and slowly, taking new things on when the time is right for me, in order to avoid overwhelm and burnout.

Julene Ewert:

My goals are always in flux. I have a small list of big things that I would LOVE to accomplish. I start with small steps that will lead to the "big thing" that I want to achieve. It's hard to be patient with the speed of this process, especially when it seems everyone else is miles ahead of me. But I know that I have to reach each milestone on my own. It's like rock climbing. You find a good hand hold that is within range, grab it and pull yourself up. One hold at a time, and suddenly you have the most amazing view!

Jodi Lebrun:

My formula for setting goals would have to be part dreaming and part small steps. I firmly believe that goals are just dreams that need to come true and that in order for them to manifest themselves we need to take small steps to help them along.

I begin by dreaming about what I'd like to accomplish - this could literally be anything from paying the bills to my next big blog post to inspire my readers or to my next e-course offering. Once I have thought about it in my head, I then take the necessary steps to make them come true. I write them down to make them real (I'm visual and need to see them written) and then I jot down some small steps that I could try to work towards them. I would then go through my potential small steps to see which one resonates the loudest with me and that's the one I would start with.
While I do veer off course once in a while, the Universe always steps in with some sign for me that reminds me of where I should be heading and that usually gets me back on track! The Universe wants us to succeed and will do what it needs to do to help us out. We just have to be willing to listen to our inner voice and be open to receiving what is coming our way. It's really that simple.

Erin Fickert-Rowland:

I am very diligent about setting goals and achieving them! I regularly evaluate "Where am I at?" and "Where do I want to go?" Though I have a long-term vision for "Where I want to go," my first task is establishing, "What is the next step?" Then, I plan out a few key steps for getting there. This gets broken down further by determining a month's worth of actions to achieve those steps, which usually gets segmented into weekly and daily task lists. Through all of this, I stay flexible and frequently re-evaluate priorities. When unexpected opportunities arise, I try to rearrange some of my plans to work them in!

I always strive for more than I can achieve. This doesn't make me feel like a failure, it keeps me motivated! Whatever I don't accomplish simply gets moved to the next list, and re-prioritized, always with the big goal remaining in focus.

Louise Gale:

Absolutely, I use the formula and process I teach in the Big Dreams, Small Wonders { http://bigdreamssmallwonders.com/ } program, where we set goals and milestones that actually stick! I stay on track by constantly reviewing where I am with a particular goal, re-adjusting if I need to for success. Most importantly celebrating each milestone along the way.

Juliette Crane: Before I set any new goals, I take time to envision what I want my daily life to look and feel like. When I first started my business, I really focused on achieving goals and getting them checked off my list. But I was exhausted and constantly living a really intense lifestyle, working way too hard each day, and not enjoying my achievements, my life or the people and things I really love. For me it's really easy to get caught up in the goals, but what matters most is enjoying my every day.

Once I envision my ideal lifestyle and have an idea of the feeling I want to have in my every day, at the beginning of each year, I set out a list of very specific goals. Inevitably, so much changes as the year goes on, so I revisit these goals every few months and realign them with where I am in that moment.

Once I have my list of goals, I prioritize each one, usually based on a rating of my passion and excitement for that goal, what it will help me achieve in my business, and whether it aligns with my lifestyle goals. I also ask myself why I want to achieve each goal…sometimes that helps me see an underlying dream or purpose that I could get to in a different way.

Since my goals and dreams often change, I only spend time on the goal/s I intend to move forward with first. That way, I don't get ahead of myself and overwhelmed before I have the chance to get started and make progress on at least one important thing.

For that first goal/s, I make a list of small steps, and then loosely schedule them into my days and weeks. I usually have one big goal at a time (like creating and launching an online course, writing and releasing an eBook etc) and balance that with my regular tasks and painting days to be sure I still have enough openness in my every day to really enjoy things.

I also make sure to have smaller weekly tasks (like blog writing or posting new artwork) to balance out the big tasks. Checking off those small tasks makes me feel accomplished. Otherwise with the big projects, I can sometimes feel like I'm never getting anywhere. Sometimes, I'll even do laundry, organize my studio or clean the kitchen if I feel like I'm not getting anything done. Those little achievements keep me feeling accomplished.

The other thing I find I need to stay on track and feel progressive is positive reinforcement, so I make sure to keep in touch with, customers, other artists and friends who provide support and lots of kind words. That's been key in keeping me focused on what really matters and inspires me to keep living my purpose.

Carrie Schmidt:

A few years ago, I took an online course called, Mondo Beyondo, about making your goals and dreams a reality. One key part is to write your goals/dreams down from basic ones to the wildest ones you can imagine. The facilitators claimed by doing this you are already setting your dreams in motion by stating your intention. I was definitely skeptical at first, but the eeriest things started happening after I wrote my list—they started coming true.

For example, I wrote "move to another part of the country." Ever since I was a child, I had always dreamed of living out West. But, we had just bought a home and had no plans to move anywhere. By a strange twist of events, we ended up moving to the Pacific Northwest a few months after I wrote it down. A total dream come true! When I wrote that, I was thinking maybe in 20 years or so. Many other items on my list have come true that I never thought would.

What has this taught me about goal setting? Write it down. Keep a list. Update your list on a daily, weekly and monthly basis. That is my formula—simple but effective for me.

I also organize goals by theme. Each week I update my artmaking, marketing, website/blog and research/learning goals. These are the areas I am choosing to focus on right now. I try to do something each week related to those areas so I am moving forward, even if it is just in a small way each week.

Valerie Hart:

I am a "list" girl and this technique works really well for me. It helps me to get things out of my head and onto paper. So I work from a "master to do list" of goals to accomplish. But on a daily basis, I only work from a post-it note. A post it note helps me from getting too overwhelmed by my master list. I can only fit one to five items on a post it note and that's plenty. It also helps to review and recognize what you "have" accomplished in your art business, not what you haven't. So often we look at our lists and see everything that still needs to be done

Elizabeth Gonzalez:

I set priorities and work toward the goals dedicating more effort to those action items that can't be postponed. If the list is too long I split it in two. One list is for the ones that can't wait and the other for the least important. Then I focus on the first list until accomplished.

Mary Nasser:

I like to break down big goals into smaller goals; this makes my goals more realistic and attainable, and makes is more likely for me to succeed in achieving them. And I think success begets success and motivates me to continue setting and working towards new goals!

One goal I set for myself in May 2011 was to finish one painting a week. Besides being specific, this goal is also measurable and tangible. To keep myself accountable, I post my newest painting on my blog each Wednesday. This formula has had great results for me: at one painting per week, I've completed more than 70 paintings since setting this goal! This achievement allowed me to set larger goals, like exhibiting in additional galleries, because now I have a larger body of work!

Amanda Fall: In the early stages of Sprout, I was so focused on the day-to-day challenges that I didn't attempt to make too many goals beyond that (research, production and sales were plenty!). Now I'm hitting that point where I'm excited to expand and am brainstorming ways that will help Sprout grow and become stronger than ever. So, that's my first point: I try to be more realistic and kind in my goal-setting now. When I'm right in the thick of it, I let myself focus on the action. There's a time for everything, and a time for expanding will come. I'm learning to trust the process.

When I'm ready to set goals, I take lots of notes. I scribble down possibilities, plans, and ideas. When I find myself writing the same thing over and over (or adding lots of underlines and stars and exclamation points), I'm certain that it's a goal I want to set.

Staying on track, then, involves lots of balance—a continual coming back to self-care, to my original motivation, to where I am in the moment and where I want to be. I practice gratitude in everything I do (or try to, at least), which helps me to keep moving forward while being grateful for what has come before.

I also need to work on patience (Right.NOW!), because one of the biggest lessons I've learned is that I definitely have a process—and sometimes it might take months or even years before I'm truly ready for an idea to come to life (Sprout was an idea in my teens; after it came back to my thought in new digital possibility, it took about a year to bring to reality). Once it IS real, I'm in the flow and all that waiting and worrying and testing and trying were so worth it. Other times things happen more quickly. I'm trying to value each method and be grateful for both.

E'Layne Koenigsberg:

I don't plan goals out far enough and absolutely need to work at posting a big calendar three months out and put target dates for tasks to be achieved. What helps me the most to achieve goals is my notebook with lists of tasks. I work on the list daily and what I don't finish gets put on the next day's list. I have different sections like a people to call list, people to pay list and a to-do list.

Katherine Quinn:

I imagine myself completing the goal… standing at my exhibition opening with lots of family and friends around me and a whole lot of red sale dots on the walls, or imagining how I would feel after getting an email or phone call to say I have been accepted into whatever my goal was and ringing my Mum to tell her the good news!!! And then I work back from there… breaking down what I need to do, and then breaking it down again until I have a clear step by step process to get to where I want to be. Sometimes there will be an unknown entity that I cannot control that might get in the way… and that is when you start in with plan B.

I like to write everything down on a daily clipboard and cross things off as they are done, seems a little over the top and my friends laugh at me but it is so helpful when I am juggling family, a day job and a creative business.

Beth Doan:

Simple answer, lists, a calendar and set time limits on how much time I spend on Facebook, Pinterest, etc. Social network is vitally important, but it can suck you into a black hole and become a timewaster, instead of a great business tool.

Again, lists and a calendar and when a custom order comes, I complete it as efficiently as possible, ahead of deadline when at all possible, even if at the time I only have that one order, because you never know when the next custom order or business opportunity will present itself and I want to be ready to roll with the next challenge in a timely and professional manner.

Mandy Saile:

Just my big desk calendar and stick-it's, they keep me on track as much as my migraine pain will allow me. I will often write an idea down and break it down into smaller parts once I started the project. Even if it's just an illustration, I will have a note on my calendar that will say 'finish 'X' this day' then maybe the day after I'll have another note that reminds me to scan 'X' into the computer, then maybe another one telling me to add 'X' to Etsy this week...I always have so many images and projects on the go at once that it's a good way to do things and keep on track.

My system still needs tweaking and I need to get more detailed past the actual completion of a goal. Because, though I never seem to have a problem of finishing projects, I do often forget to follow right through to the marketing of them and this is something I am aware that must work on.

I think part of my problem is that because I am short on time because of my headaches, once I am back in working form & back in the studio, I am always so anxious to start on the next image or doll or whatever it may be. Though my system is far from perfect, it does seem to get refined and work a bit better each year. And, I do feel very proud of myself when I hear someone say 'wow you're so prolific and get so much done', because that really is for me been quite tough.

For more days than not honestly, you'll find me laying down with heat and ice packs for 30 minutes or so, then getting up and working for as long as I can until the pain gets soo bad that I feel like I am going to throw up or like my head is going to split open, then I lay down again and then get up to work again, etc etc. This is a common routine for me and sometimes when I've had head pain for 14 days straight, I start to feel tuckered out and I need to break and regroup myself.

BUT I am not meaning to complain too much for my head pain has taught me such gratitude in a roundabout sort of way and they force me to slow down and to really really enjoy the small little lovelies life offers. Like I mentioned, I really do wonder where I would be in my business if I could operate like a normal pain-free person…so I always tell people, if your migraine/pain-free, get off your butt and go go go, you have no excuses.

YOUR TURN:

Do you have a formula for setting goals? How do you stay on track for achieving your goal?

Question #28

When you are facing a dilemma in your business, what are the steps you take to solve the problem?

Be brave. Take risks. Nothing can substitute experience.

Paulo Coelho

I work my dilemmas through the following four steps:

Step Away –

Work on something else –

Regroup –

Get Honest – is this thing really worth my time and energy to continue in.

Case Study: Kickstarter project vs This book

I had started a kickstarter project. Kickstarter is a company that offers a way to fund creative projects by setting a goal and pitching your idea to everyone you know in your circle and virtually to get funding for completing your project. The typical fund drive is 30 days. At about 20 days in I have reached just 26% of my goal and decided to cancel the kickstarter project. I instead created a PDF of the project and have been successful with Plan B.

This book you hold in your hands started as an idea at the beginning of 2012. I had completed Kelly Rae Roberts' first ever ecourse called Flying Lessons (most of the people in this project are part of the original alumni group) and KNEW I wanted to find a way to work with all of these talented people that I met through the course. So I came up with the idea called the 101010 Project. 10 women with online businesses would answer 10 soul stirring questions in the midst of a 10 day blog hop. It would be done in 3 phases so that we would ultimately come up with a 30 day journey into transforming our businesses as well as helping others to do the same.
Session 1 went fairly smoothly. But by session 2 I was having a bit more trouble getting 10 participants. I am so very grateful for the 7 that were able to keep moving the project forward.

But by the end of session 2 I was ready to give up. Here I go again with these big lofty ideas!

Until...

I got BRAVE and I just began emailing as many people as I could to see if they would be interested. Plan B came through once again and I HAVE TO SAY that the finished project is even BETTER that I ever imagined.

Lisa Wilson:

The first thing I do, no matter how big or small the dilemmas is, is to take a breath. When I'm facing what I consider to be a problem, I almost always start breathing shallower. It is important that I find my breath before any answers.

The next thing I do, as in every other situation, is to shift perspective. If the computer locks up, it's perhaps not a problem…it's an opportunity to go outside for a breath of fresh air.

I don't wear rose-colored glasses; not everything is all peachy keen. I get as pissed as the next person when I lose hours of work that I forgot to save. But it is what it is. If I want to keep my self sane and healthy, and my business running smoothly, the time-proven best option is to flow around the rocks in my path, not stay stuck behind them just getting upset.

Catherine Just:

I do several things when I am facing a dilemma in my business:

1. I check in with the people around me that I trust the most to get feedback and suggestions.

2. I sit still and allow the answer to come from within me.

3. I sleep on it.
4. I take a photo walk with my iPhone and get out of the house and look and notice the world around me. It helps me to get more present, helps me calm down the racing mind, and calms me down.

Kat Sloma:

Usually I let myself sit with the problem. My natural reaction is respond immediately to problems, but in reality I often have time to think about the response. When I take the time to think about it, usually new options for a solution will appear. I will journal about the problem, look at it from a few angles, and then formulate a plan to resolve it. Once I've had a chance to think it through calmly, the problem and solution don't usually seem as big as they did initially.

Nataša May:

When there's a dilemma I write down my thoughts first. Writing is the easiest way for me to get clear on my thoughts. Then I sleep on it. Everything seems so much more manageable after I had a good night sleep. And I never lose the sense of "I can fix this." It's actually my motto while painting as well. I cannot mess up SO much that I cannot fix it. And that thought alone has gotten me out of a slump many times.

And I have a rule to always be nice and diplomatic when corresponding with people. That doesn't mean I don't get angry but I cannot afford to be mean to people even though I sometimes want to be. So I stay clear of accusations and just state the facts and hopefully we can try to find a solution together.

Julene Ewert:

Try not to take the dilemmas I face personally. When something is printed wrong, or a buyer is unhappy with a product, or someone says they dislike my paintings, I try hard not to let it get me down. If it really hits me wrong, I have a pity party. Really, it works on so many levels. You get to let it out and then you can move on.

My graphic design background helps me be the professional. When faced with a problem I focus on the professional side and make it right. I tell myself, how would I like to be treated in this situation? We all want to be treated with respect and want our feelings heard. Make it right and learn.

Erin Fickert-Rowland:

When facing a dilemma, the very first thing I do, is stay calm and speak positively to myself. I need to understand the problem and start to plan to solve it. Once I have thoughtfully examined a pressing issue, I will discuss it with a trusted consultant. I will gather opinions and advice, and begin to research solutions. I determine my available resources of money and time, and start to establish a plan of action. Throughout this process, I remind myself to stay calm and positive, because my proposed solution may not work the first time!

Louise Gale:

I think the initial reaction when something doesn't go to plan is to panic! But I have learned that everything happens for a reason and can be solved, so I always take a step back and evaluate all the areas that this effects, re-focus on my bigger picture goals and how I can make any small changes necessary to get to a solution.

Kim Gann:

I research ways to solve it, tackle it head on and make the changes I need to make in order to continue success

Carrie Schmidt:

First, I remind myself that anything is possible, that there is a solution for anything. Having faith and a positive outlook that the universe is on my side is key for me to stay my course despite challenges.

Then, I seek out people I trust to listen and to offer advice, especially my parents. People are great resources—sometimes it is as simple as just asking.

If that doesn't work, I research online. I love reading about people's experiences if I cannot talk to them personally.

Thirdly, I listen to my intuition and remind myself to have patience. Believing that things have a way of revealing themselves at the right time helps me stay calm.

Amanda Fall:

I'm a praying person, so I will pray that whatever I do reflects a divine glow, that my motivation comes from a higher place and that I am just a messenger. This helps me find perspective. I practice deep listening to see what practical steps might need to be taken.

Depending on the situation, I may ask for help from a trusted friend who's been there. I may go back to my favorite, the list-making method, which helps me clarify and see what I couldn't see before.

In all things, I am trying to practice honesty, because so often I've found that these dilemmas stem from misunderstandings or a break-down in communication. Being up-front and honest always brings clarity (as long as you're careful to speak from a place of calm, strength and kindness).

E'Layne Koenigsberg:

My first step is to step back and breathe. I find I can get too emotional about some "dramas" and have found it's never good to act from a place of emotion. Our business recently had another craft business out and out lie about our business and said we were copying them when they were copying us. We were livid and friends were advising us to get an attorney. Being more of a peace maker than litigiously prone, we decided to take the high road and ignore the whole situation and stay focused on our wonderful business. Their attempts to bad mouth us fell on deaf ears and they were seen by the art community as being mean spirited. If we had acted from an emotional place the matter would have escalated and used up precious time, energy and money.

Mandy Saile:

I usually sit down with my sweetie and talk things through with him. He is an excellent project manager for the government and he has a very no nonsense/common sense about things. I can get very emotional and hyper about things and he calms me right down and helps me see how things really are...he helps balance me out.

I also, try to trust my gut while making sure fear isn't playing into my decisions, which is sometimes tricky. My biggest dilemma is often budget issues. I operate my business on a shoe-string budget really and opportunities and chances I see other artists making often aren't an option for me. Especially when in the past I have sprung for opportunities that should have worked out and they just didn't. So when that happens time and time again, it makes one a little more cautious.

But, I've come to trust my own decisions and to settle in a little more comfortably with my limitations and to let go of all of the often quickly offered 'you should do this and that's". I think it helps too to stay as inspired as possible. There are days where I feel down, so on those days I stay off the internet and social networks, etc, I avoid the easy temptation to compare myself to everyone else. On positive and strong days, I find inspiring stories and artists where I can say to myself 'hey I can try that too' or 'I am good enough to do that as well', the key is knowing when to do what, ha ha.

I also have 4 big bulletin boards in my studio that are jam-packed with image concepts and sketches etc and on those days where things are feeling sticky I will put everything aside and get straight back to the root of it all, which is the artwork itself…I allow myself the whole day or maybe the whole week or sometimes even the whole month to just create and not worry about any of the other stuff. Creating always makes things very clear and having these bulletin boards in full view is a constant reminder that I have oodles of creating to do and somehow that always calms me and acts as a reminder that I can jump right back to the root of it all and that it's there that all will be okay…

YOUR TURN:
When you facing a dilemma in your business, what are the steps you take to solve the problem?

Question #29

What kind of attributes do you look for in someone you want to collaborate with?

Let this truth go as deep in you as possible: that life is already here, arrived. You are standing on the goal. Don't ask about the path.

-
Osho

I actually wrote a workbook about the collaboration process. I have found that you need to move very carefully and deliberately when collaborating.

Here are the attributes I look for:

-someone who is good at generating ideas
-someone with similar personality and energy
-someone who is hard working
-someone who is taking risks/challenges in their own business

Lisa Wilson:

Honesty, kindness, commitment, and flexibility. An open-minded sense of lightheartedness about it all is crucial. I don't need someone to tell me the 'the realities' of a situation. My fear-based mind has already created all of the worse-case scenarios. I need support, honest feedback, and laughter.

Kat Sloma:

This is an important question! I think you have to take on collaborations carefully, especially ones that will involve a big time and money commitment. You need to be able to speak openly about your goals and desires, make decisions jointly, and, if it's not working, be able to dissolve the collaboration.

What initially may seem like an ideal collaboration may not pan out, maybe due to differences of opinion, direction or approach, and you need to have a strong relationship to talk openly about how to work through the issues. Having a clearly stated goal, along with up-front agreements on decision making processes and financial arrangements (if any), is critical to a good collaboration. If you find you can't talk through these items openly at the beginning with someone, you probably don't want to enter into collaboration with them.

Julene Ewert:

I want someone that is as driven as I am. I look for someone focused and reliable. Style is not as important. Instead it is personality, and the ability to have fun while working towards a goal that is paramount. I collaborate with those who are honest about telling me what they want and what they think, while still lifting me up.

Erin Fickert-Rowland:

I am always excited to work with someone who is positive, dependable, hard-working, trustworthy, honest, sincere, and knowledgeable about their work. I do not enjoy working with people who are focused on themselves, communicate poorly, do not follow through with commitments, and are quick to abandon a project or a person for a "bigger fish."

Louise Gale:

I think fun to work with is a must and reliability! I really value doing what I say I will do so this is an attribute in someone else that I will always look for. I really love to brainstorm and talk about different ideas so someone who gets fired up just like me to see how we can create something new is so inspiring. Creating something and seeing it grow and be successful is amazing, but doing that with another creative soul is even more awesome!

Kim Gann:

Positive outlook. Someone who knows rules are made to be broken. Creative spirit. Someone I feel connected to through our art and creativity

Cindy Silverstein:

When the time comes that I am ready to collaborate with someone on a project, such as an e-course, a book, or a workshop, I will seek out someone with whom I feel a spark, a soul connection. We will light up whenever we see each other, and when we talk about and work on a project.

I will want that person to have integrity, passion for their work, a desire to make a contribution to humanity...someone with a positive
attitude, a desire to share their creative and artistic ideas, and a strong wish to empower and uplift those with whom they work, and the people they teach.

I would chose someone who is on a path of self-knowledge, someone who is a seeker of truth and is brave enough to be open to letting go of self-limiting beliefs, one who is growing in self-awareness and is available to listening and learning...someone who is talented and creative, great at teamwork and brainstorming...someone whose gifts will fill in the areas where my talents might not be so strong, and the reverse.

I would keep alert for someone who has enthusiasm for sharing their wealth of knowledge, not only of art and techniques, but of personal growth and the awareness of the importance of developing a strong sense of self-worth in order to grow as an artist, and the know-how to help people grow in this way... a person who is flexible and is willing to speak for their ideas, and willing to let go of even the most cherished idea when necessary.

Of course no one could display such perfection all the time, yet I would want someone who would at least see the beauty in these attributes and
possess a good selection of them.

Laura Gaffke:

Someone open minded who doesn't let their ego get in the way of creating good work. Someone adaptable, who has different skills than me so we balance each other, someone who challenges me and pushes me in new directions just by being who they are.

Elizabeth Gonzalez:

Trustworthy, creative, open minded, positive, honest and hard working.

Amanda Fall:

Again, kindhearted honesty is key. The ability to speak up for what we believe is right is so important—and can be a tremendous place of growth, if it comes from gentleness and openness, and if both people are willing to listen. I love to collaborate with someone whose strengths complement my weaknesses, and vice versa.

E'Layne Koenigsberg:

In the book The Four Agreements don Miguel Ruiz gives four principles to practice in order to create love and happiness in life. They are:

1. Be Impeccable with your Word
2. Don't Take Anything Personally
3. Don't Make Assumptions
4. Always Do Your Best.

I personally aspire to keep these agreements and I look for these attributes in the people with whom I collaborate.

Mandy Saile:

I need to work with fellow animal lovers, that is pretty much key in almost all aspects of my life and business. I also need to work with people who are positive and happy to be working on whatever the project is we are working on.

I need respect for my talent and I need my fellow collaborators to be professional, to keep to their end of things, to be open and willing to communicate the whole entire way. But some flexibility is key, because again, my head pain factors in and I can only sign on with people who understand that it's a big factor in my life at the time being.

So in short, I am great at super tight deadlines but if I can avoid them I will. Ultimately, I need to really connect with the person and feel like though we may be completely different, they respect and 'get' me and my work and vice versa.

YOUR TURN:

What kind of attributes do you look for in someone you want to collaborate with?

Question #30

Describe a time when you took a big leap forward in your business. What were the lessons learned and what were the shifts you made in how you view your business as a result?

Let go of the things you fear to lose. Die to your attachments.
Free yourself from everything you think you are and embrace the
truth that you are abundant, eternal, fearless and worth being loved.

-

Jackson Kiddard

In 2012 I finally decided to take the leap and become certified as a life coach. Ten years this notion was percolating within me. And then finally the excuses fell away. Money no longer became the hindrance because I did not let it hinder the YES any longer. Time constraints fell away because I had run out of excuses; I saw that somehow I was able to find the time for other things I wanted to do. Fear moved out of the way because I suddenly let go of things I thought other people wanted me to do and began listening to the voice inside me.

Lessons learned:

- I had to listen to and get comfortable with the longer view on things.

- I had to listen to the voice inside me

- I had to be willing to let go of what I think my business is supposed to look like.

- I had to let go of energy draining tasks that would hinder me being able to accomplish the goal

Lisa Wilson: I love reflecting on this question because it makes me realize how many leaps I've actually taken!

Perhaps one of the biggest leaps has happened rather recently, and somewhat unexpectedly. After years of debating how, when, and if I was going to offer online classes through LifeUnity, I finally committed to a life coach that I was going to make it a priority to get one running.

Within a few weeks, I had a rough outline, my website mostly updated, and two promotional videos made. One very late night, I hit publish on a post announcing a class I hadn't even finished designing. The next day, I promoted the Encaustic Experience: Beginner's Mind all over Facebook and Twitter and had people signing up almost immediately. I was beyond thrilled!

The reality of the situation didn't hit me until about 2 days before the class was supposed to open – when I still had a PDF to finish, videos to render, and a web page to update...and that was just to be done with week one of the class.

Needless to say, the next six weeks of the class were a whirlwind of countless late nights, carry-out dinners for the family, and thrilling ups and downs as I saw inspirational creative breakthroughs from the participants all while my computer was locking up and mysteriously deleting posts.

I quickly learned how much behind-the-scenes work goes into creating and running a class, and how many hours of creation are required when you want to give your fellow travelers the most thorough experience possible. I wasn't willing to sacrifice – when I had an idea or when the participants had a question, I would follow through no matter how much time it took. I owed it to both them and to myself to commit to the class and the experience.

What surprised me the most – and I may be giving away some trade secret here – is that I wasn't alone. Almost every other online teacher to whom I talked said they did exactly the same thing (to varying degrees): they simply put it out there that they were leading a class and did the design after the announcement! I think we can often get bogged down in the details of design. Sometimes, we just need to outwardly commit to make the idea "real"...and then just do what needs to be done to make it happen.

Since then, my entire conceptualization of my business has changed. I've experienced both the slow drift of thinking about ideas and simply doing a bit here and there and the adrenaline-fueled rush of constant work and expression. I know that I don't want to permanently have my business (nor my life) in either mode. I love the rush of offering thoughts and wisdom and art to the world, but I also crave and require the silence of withdrawing and being simply with myself.

It is like my breath – I need to exhale, to share, and to give back; I need to inhale, to take in, and to be inspired; and I need the pauses in between it all.

My business is growing from this experience, evolving into something very unique indeed. I am making it a priority and a practice to have both my life and my business reflect exactly what I encourage others to do – to live mindfully, express creatively, and do it all while getting the kids fed and the laundry done.

Katie Clemons:

The biggest leap for our personal lives and work began one year ago. My husband and I started restoring an old airplane hangar, turning part of it into a teeny home and office. We're still building, piece by piece. Building has been a test of patience and endurance all in one.

I don't have as much time as I'd like to work on my business. It's really forced me to be streamlined and smart with the time that I do have available. There's just not a lot of time to surf the internet or tweet.

Kat Sloma:

I think one of my biggest leaps forward in my business was when I moved to my new website. I knew that I would need to move from my Blogger blog to a "real" website for my business. It wasn't possible to do everything I needed and wanted to do with a blog! Originally I thought I would figure out how to create the website myself since I have a technical background, but as I was trying to run classes and create new material, I realized I could not do it. I took the plunge and paid someone to do set up my website for me. It has been my single biggest expense to date, but was worth every penny. I got exactly what I needed in a time frame that would not have been remotely possible on my own. And with so much less stress!

It was going through the process of creating my website that I finally realized I was running a business. It was weird to hear my designer jokingly call me "boss" and to discover I truly was his boss. I contracted him to do this work, and I needed to be clear on what I wanted and make sure I was satisfied. I am no longer just a consumer in this world, but a small business owner generating value and reinvesting in other businesses. Wow!
That realization also helped me shift from feeling awkward that I was charging money for what I create, to being proud of creating something of value and participating in the economy. That's pretty cool!

As I take on a new project, I've started to look at what makes sense to pay others for and what I want to do myself. I'm still doing a lot of my own work, but if it's a task I have no energy for and there is someone who has a service to do that task for me, I'll seriously consider hiring them. I can do more of what I love to do – photography, writing, creating and teaching classes – when I hire someone to do the behind-the-scenes tasks for me.

Nataša May:

My biggest leap so far was the decision to teach an on-line workshop. I had to learn so much in the technology department before I could even start filming the workshop. Luckily following directions and finding solutions to any problem is my strong suit but that doesn't mean I wasn't stressed out because of it. There was a lot of research involved to put the on-line workshop together and I was surprised I couldn't find all the information in one place. I decided to put my findings in a PDF and share it with everyone for free to make it easier for everyone else searching for the same information. You can find it here:
http://natashamay.blogspot.com/p/free-tips.html

I also had to do some soul searching to find the balance between how much I value my own work, how much I wanted to give and how much I thought people were willing to pay. It was a battle for me in regards to whether I want to charge more but get less students or charge less and get more students.

Julene Ewert:

I started my business selling handmade jewelry. It was an incredible money-maker and it pushed me to try full-time self employment. But when sales started to slow, and others around me started to sell similar products, I knew that I couldn't keep doing the same thing and continue to be successful.

I've learned that with any business, there are cycles. It also taught me that I need to create items that are completely me. I started painting and creating mixed media works that reflect my values and tap into my own spirit. I remember the first art and craft show that I did not sell any handmade jewelry. I only brought my art. I told myself, "please let me sell just one thing...and I hope no one laughs at me." That day I did sell artwork, and people said they loved it! It was an incredible day and it gave me a feeling I wish I could bottle and pull out when I need a boost. It's the feeling that you know you are doing the right thing.

Erin Fickert-Rowland:

Now is that time for Elysian Studios. I have been working a little over two years on building this business, and it has involved a lot of learning curves! The biggest lessons I have learned are:

Be fearless. Make mistakes and learn from them. Always get better. Get the right tools for the job you want to get done right.

I have decided not to be afraid to put myself out there. Everyone makes mistakes, and I am no different. I admit a mistake, correct it, and continue to push forward. I have taken the time and money necessary to invest in my business, establishing the important building blocks it needs for long-term success. I have not begun this endeavor with a large sum of money, loans, or investors, so I am content with the slow evolution that is required. I view my business like a beautifully flowing river: I look forward and am exhilarated by the promise of fresh water coming, I look backward and smile at the memory of the water that nourished me, and I look down and am content with the possibilities that are continuously flowing.

Louise Gale:

Last year I decided to embark on formal training to become a life coach. This was a huge leap and my main reason for doing this was to be able to incorporate these philosophies into my current and future work. This was a great learning experience for me on a personal level as well and has really helped me approach my business in a new free flowing way. I learned a lot about the energy of our thoughts and I worked hard to incorporate this into my everyday life and my approach to business. I now offer sessions

{ http://louisegale.com/work-with-me/ } to help other creative souls learn about their energy levels and how this affects their own business and life.

Carrie Schmidt:

I recently invested in hiring a web designer to launch my first professional website. This was a turning point for me--I finally decided I deserved a website and that I was an artist. I was surprised how this shifted my feelings and confidence about me as an artist, as well as served as a huge motivation to keep creating.

This has had a domino effect in other areas of my art life. I've decided to move my art studio into a room in our home, as well as having my current detached garage studio. I'm finally realizing that my art deserves a prime location in our home, in my life, and that it is a part of me that I need to embrace. This is about me saying that I deserve this.

Before I didn't think I deserved to take up a room in our home for my art, but I am finally letting myself claim its importance in my life. I've embraced a new sense of ownership I have about my life as an artist and am making choices from a different place now, one that finally takes me seriously.

Valerie Hart:

In 2008 I was working in a corporate position doing marketing, branding and web design. I was laid off 9 months after the financial crisis hit, and I decided to take some time and re-evaluate my career. I was always interested in doing my own art and art licensing, but I had still not found my art style. It takes time, energy and practice to develop art and to see your style emerge.

Taking a few online courses like Kelly Rae Roberts' Flying Lessons really helped jump start the process for me. The biggest lesson I learned is that you just have to keep creating art. Turn off the TV, forget about the dishes and laundry and just keep creating art. If you don't like a piece of art that you created, put it in the closet and start again. Not every one of your works is going to be a masterpiece. The more you do, the better you get at it.

Amanda Fall:

Actually . . . I'm working on this right now, behind the scenes. I'm developing a brand new website for Sprout via WordPress. I'm ready to take over the reins and have more control over what happens on my site. It's a little scary, being the one in charge, but so empowering. I'm excited to take this next step in committing to my business and myself. Sprout is here to stay, and it deserves a beautiful new home that better represents its gorgeous insides. It's time for the "outside" to match the inside.

Sprout has grown so much from its beginning stages, and so have I, but the website hasn't changed much. I finally took a step back and realized that full commitment means honoring my product and taking (another) leap of faith, knowing that grace will catch me . . . as it always has.

e'Layne Koenigsberg:

I recently spent a year rebranding my business and had a new website built. My business was not under one umbrella...it was not easily understood by my customers. I make original art, have a production wing for wholesaling with my partner, write articles for Stampington Publication, blog...and there was no consistency in branding.

I created the domain www.artbyelayne with wordpress.org and all the different hats I wear in my business are now under that umbrella. Taking this step has actually helped me understand my business better. When I had several websites and several blogs all scattered about it made me feel extremely disorganized and overwhelmed. The task of rebranding made me look strategically at my business and define it for my customers...as well as for myself...why I'm in business.

Beth Doan:

The biggest leap forward in my business was last Fall. Another Maine Etsy Shop owner, who also is a partner with Maine Jewelry & Art Gallery, Bangor Maine, found me on Etsy and invited me to consign with their Gallery through the Holiday Season and I did pretty well. I also had the best Holiday season with my Etsy Shop since I opened in March 2009. It was a huge boost to my confidence!

My biggest lesson learned was having a good quality product is not enough if you are building your business on Etsy or anywhere online. You need good photos and good tags for your customers to find you and to engage. I now view myself as a businesswoman and it feels good. Really, really good. I have learned that, upper most, if I am going to get my business to the next level, my next goal needs to be consistent, good social networking.

Mandy Saile:

I think my leap into blogging was a really big leap. Before that my art world felt so very very small and limited. Blogging has opened me up, it makes me want to work harder because I want to have new work to show my lovely group of 'fans' and it just keeps me positive about everything really.

On any given grumpy day I just have to browse my blog to be quickly reminded of the enchanted life I lead. To start a blog and open up to the online world, to trust that people would connect, that people would ultimately be kind, well it was a big deal.

Now blogging is just part of my day and I can't see myself without it. So far blogging has not offered up any negative experiences.

Next would be my Etsy shop, opening up an online shop, having the courage to believe that other people might want to spend their hard earned money on my work, well that felt like a big leap too. I would be honored if you read my interview for the 'Courage To Fly' blog hop; it talks all about my courageous leaps forward and what it means to live a creative life:

http://bijouswhimsy.blogspot.ca/2011/04/courage-to-fly.html
.

Because of the blog and the online shop, I have learned that people are interested in me and in my work, there are people out there inspired by my life and by my artwork and that feels like such a precious gift…it makes me want to continue with it all and to keep striving to move forward to bigger and better things and that it's okay to do so…it's okay to lead an abundant life because the people who I really want in my life are going to be the people who want to see that abundance happen for me.

It's taken awhile to settle into the fact that I am allowed to market my artwork, that it doesn't mean I am full of myself, that my business and the marketing part of it is just me trying to spread my hard earned talents and stories and dreams and that I am allowed to do so as much as anyone else out there, especially since my message is one of joy, kindness, light and connection. I've also learned that patience is key. It takes awhile to find one's online tribe. It takes awhile sometimes for those 'real' connections to be found. But once they are, oh boy they can be so so uplifting and wonderful. I am trusting in the old adage that

        'all good things takes time'

        and that I must

'Never Give Up For That Is Just The Place And Time That The Tide Will Turn'

I know I will never turn away from my dream of creating beautiful artwork and running a successful creative business in the middle of my own beautiful successful rabbit sanctuary. Life is so so precious, and living a creative life is such a huge gift, Oh boy, I could go on and on, ha ha...but I'll stop here and just say...

Thanks so so much for your time everyone...

                    Be Kind, Be Joyful and Be Inspired

YOUR TURN:

Describe a time when you took a big leap forward in your business. What were the lessons learned and what were the shifts you made in how you view your business as a result?

Conclusion:

So many valuable lessons to be learned through open and authentic conversations. Questions offer a means to look at your business/creative endeavors in an "outside of the box" fashion, especially those questions that have a non traditional approach to describing your business/creative endeavors in terms of color or animals or even inanimate objects.

A plethora of discussion was done on the value of collaboration coupled with heartbreaking and celebratory accounts from behind the scenes of these little communities which are often tucked away in the "no discussion" zone.

I want to thank you for taking the time to move through the questions and through the stories of the many talented women and the beautiful businesses they have birthed through love, passion, necessity.

I truly hope that you walk away from these pages with fresh perspective on the way you want to move through your passions, your vision and/or your current undertakings.

I would love it if you share on the website and/or at Amazon.com your reviews of this book.

Free Gifts For you....

Robin Norgren:
How to Start a Creativity Movement
http://www.robinnorgrenstudios.blogspot.com

e'Layne Koenigsberg:
Techniques of a Thriving Artist
http://forms.aweber.com/form/97/1513981897.htm

Kat Sloma:

- Exploring with a Camera - A free monthly series celebrating the wonder and excitement of exploring the world with a camera in your hands. No "challenges" or "assignments" here! Just the fun of exploring a new photography topic every month and the invitation to join.

- Photo-Heart Connection - A free monthly series to develop a practice that will deepen the connection between your photos and your heart and soul. By joining in, you will develop relationships with other like-minded photographers searching for the same photo-heart connection.

- Basic Composition Camera Companion - Sign up for the Kat Eye News, a twice-monthly email newsletter full of inspiration on photography and the creative journey, and receive this handy pocket-sized guide to basic photographic composition.

Amanda Fall:

Enter code SPARK to receive any one issue of Sprout for free at
http://sproutonlinemagazine.com

Juliette Crane:

Mixed Media Tutorials: Here is the link to all of my videos:
http://vimeo.com/user6273546/videos

Jodi Lebrun:

Art Share-a-Palooza 2011 my first e-book (which you can get for free at www.creativelifebydesign.com)

Natasa May:

Tips on how to create an online course
http://natashamay.blogspot.com/p/free-tips.html

Book/E-course Recommendations:

e'Layne Koenigsberg:

Kelly Rae Roberts - Flying Lessons
Kelly Rae Roberts and Beth Nicholls - Hello Soul Hello Business

Mandy Saile:

1. How Much Joy Can You Stand by Suzanne Falter-Barns
2. You Can't Afford The Luxury Of A Negative Thought by Peter McWilliams
3. Living In The Light by Shakti Gawain

Kat Sloma:

- **What to Remember When Waking: The Disciplines of an Everyday Life** by David Whyte. I loved listening to Whyte's voice on this audio CD. He weaves his poetry in with his story of embarking on a career to be a poet, and how that generalizes to all of us who are taking steps into a new unknown.
- **Trust the Process: An Artist's Guide to Letting Go** by Shaun McNiff. This book discussed creativity from so many different angles. Every time I picked it up to read I was inspired and nodding my head, "Yes!" McNiff gives a lot of practical exercises sprinkled through the book, but they are so deftly woven in the text you hardly notice they are there. This book may appeal to visual artists more than either of the two above.
- **Simple Abundance: A Daybook of Comfort and Joy** by Sarah Ban Breathnach. There is so much good in this book! I never read it daily, but would read several days at a time when I came to this book. There were topics that I didn't resonate with (like the desire for a perfectly organized

linen closet, ugh!) but there were many more topics that did resonate with me. There is much inspiration in this book to help you reconnect with who you are in the midst of a busy life as a modern woman.

Amanda Fall:

DESIRE TO INSPIRE: USING CREATIVE PASSION TO TRANSFORM THE WORLD, by **Christine Mason Miller**

INNER EXCAVATION: EXPLORE YOUR SELF THROUGH PHOTOGRAPHY, POETRY AND MIXED MEDIA, by **Liz Lamoreux**

ART SAVES: STORIES, INSPIRATION AND PROMPTS SHARING THE POWER OF ART, by **Jenny Doh**

Elizabeth Gonzalez:

"Sources of Inspiration" by Carolyn Genders.
http://www.amazon.co.uk/Sources-Inspiration-Ceramics-Applied-Arts/dp/0713670983

"Collage Journeys" by Jane Davies
http://www.amazon.com/Collage-Journeys-Practical-Creating-Personal/dp/0823099512

Lisa Wilson:

The Art of Possibility: Transforming Professional and Personal Life by Rosamund Stone Zander and Benjamin Zander

Buddha Standard Time: Awakening to the infinite possibilities of now by Lama Surya Das

Sacred Economics: Money, Gift, & Society in the age of transition by Charles Eisenstein

Juliette Crane:

The FIRE STARTER SESSIONS by Danielle Laporte

http://www.amazon.com/gp/product/030795210X/ref=as_li_qf_sp_asin_tl?ie=UTF8&camp=1789&creative=9325&creativeASIN=030795210X&linkCode=as2&tag=owlsandothera-20

The Art of Nonconformity by Chris Guillebeau

http://www.amazon.com/gp/product/B0042FZWC0/ref=as_li_qf_sp_asin_tl?ie=UTF8&camp=1789&creative=9325&creativeASIN=B0042FZWC0&linkCode=as2&tag=owlsandothera-20

Capacity by Theo Ellsworth

http://www.amazon.com/gp/product/0979960924/ref=as_li_qf_sp_asin_tl?ie=UTF8&camp=1789&creative=9325&creativeASIN=0979960924&linkCode=as2&tag=owlsandothera-20

Robin Norgren:

The Big Leap by Gay Hendricks

Stretching Lessons by Sue Bender

This Time I Dance by Tama Kieves

Bios of the Beautiful People you Met Within These Pages

Kelly Thiel found clay in 1999. Interested in all things creative, she grew up with an artistic mother on a small farm in rural Georgia, where she developed her love of playing in the mud. Those formative years influenced her greatly, and since then, she has always been involved in the arts.

A couple of years after graduating from Virginia Tech, Kelly moved to Charleston, SC and began actively pursuing her creative interests. She traveled around the country to study with different artists, like Tom Coleman and Lisa Clague, and to further her knowledge of the clay. She has shown her award-winning sculptures in regional and national exhibitions, and currently participates with the American Craft Council retail shows each year. Several of her sculptures are included in the Art Buzz, Collection 2011, and an art book dedicated to the visual arts. Kelly has also recently expanded to offer select pieces in bronze.

While Kelly is known for her clay work, she has always sketched and painted on the side, when time permitted. She finds that working in the different mediums is inspiring and freeing, and the influence from one carries over into the next.

With a studio on John's Island, SC Kelly is able to stay connected with the natural environment, and has a wonderful view of pasture and pond, with many trees and birds.

Website
Blog
Twitter
Facebook

Stephanie Amos aka SAMOS is a multimedia artist who creates unique abstract figures in bronze, delicate ceramics in bright, funky colors and colorful abstract paintings in oil, acrylic, and watercolor. She is a Colorado Native that grew up in the beautiful mountains of Salida. Stephanie received her BA from Mesa State College in Grand Junction and studied abroad to further her art education in Florence, Italy.

"Drawing was my first love, and then I discovered many doors that lead to endless creations of the imagination. It's the process that I am drawn to, whether it's starting with a blank canvas, and a ball of clay or a sheet of wax. Each medium I work in has its own unique process, and it's those differences that make it difficult for me to choose just one to work with. I have been painting abstracts since the early 90's. It wasn't until I went back to school that I started to explore other avenues. In 1999, I studied at NYU in Florence, Italy. It was there that sculpture and photography became my main interests and I developed a greater admiration for art history."

Website
Blog
Twitter
Etsy

Hello creative souls!

My name is Leanne Wargowsky. I am the creator, dreamer, artist and writer behind **From Chaos Comes Happiness**. Born, raised, and still living in the Chicago land area, my creative adventure started long before my college days, where I majored in art & theater. While life paved a different road for me (I ultimately spent the past 20 years with a career in health care), I always dreamt of following my heart and creating.

I dipped my toes in a creative life back in July of 2009, when I first discovered the "Land of Blogging". I was so inspired by the amazing talents of so many creative souls in the world, and had an overwhelming desire to share *my* stories and outlook with others. My support system is wide and deep, with a husband and two daughters who encourage my true self to come out each moment of my days. So, with butterflies in my stomach, I jumped in and began my blog. Sharing my thoughts, fears, and dreams was just the beginning. A return to my creative roots had begun, and I loved every minute of it.

In 2011, my professional future in health care took a back seat when I began **From Chaos Comes Happiness.** I am proud to offer a wide range of creative and whimsical art pieces to inspire a happy life. From hand painted mixed media work, to note cards, prints, bookmarks, magnets and jewelry. Each and every part of my collection shares my inspiring and motivating outlook on life.

THIS is ME. This is my life. Chaotic. Creative. And, oh-so Good.

LINKS:
Blog
Facebook
Etsy

Alease M. McClenningham considers herself a collage architect. She has always been drawn to the process of creating beautiful things from found objects and sees inspiration all around. Her passion is to breathe new life into bits and pieces of old, worn and forgotten elements and incorporate them into her work. She enjoys implying the rough outline of a story with the images she chooses and by the bits of ephemera she adds.

As a mixed-media artist, Alease participated in several exhibitions. Wishing to market her artistic endeavors, she found little advice available. This coupled with her passion for education – she tracked her online marketing & branding journey and founded The School of Creative Business.

As an expert, Alease lends knowledge to the press, editorials and serves as a subject-matter expert. She is a sought-after presenter in the areas of creative marketing, personal image, branding and fashion.

As an educator, Alease is committed to her students' education, furthering their exposure and considers their success a direct reflection of herself.

School of Creative Business
Website
Facebook
Twitter

God has blessed Sonya with a rare gift of conceptual vision backed with solid design skills. She has more than a decade of experience delivering print, web, and multi-media projects to clients. Sonya's willingness to become fully involved in a project, from concept to completion, ensures that every client project has a successful outcome. Sonya is a fashion graduate of O'More College of Design and a continuing student at Nashville State, where she studied visual communications. A dual platform graphic designer with the ability to master most design tools and media.

For many years Sonya worked in the fashion & newspaper industry. She worked as a buyer/manager for boutiques & mass merchants. Sonya's love of cowboy boots and western wear comes from studying this culture while buying this unique apparel for a mass boot merchant in Tennessee. Later, working for a publishing giant, Sonya mastered the art of publishing from advertising to editorial while creating her business eastwind productions.

The love of her children inspired Sonya to petition her *FATHER* to care for the gift of her children and on July 14 - 2008; Sonya quit the best paying job she ever had. With a huge mortgage and car note ... Sonya began her journey of learning to depend completely on him.

Sonya also has a natural love of photography & gardening. Early childhood exposure to French and European culture provides the foundation for Sonya's unique design sense and style.
Sonya enjoys collaborating with her creator and is simply blow away by HIS power, each and every day.

Website

Jean Simrose: I've loved creating things as long as I can remember. I learned to sew, knit and crochet when I was very young. My sisters and I were always doing crafts of some kind.

I always loved jewelry and when I moved to Seattle in 2005 I took a Silversmithing course at a local college. I've continued to take classes and make jewelry ever since.

I started by making gifts for my family and friends. As my passion increased, I experimented with different mediums and made more jewelry. I started my blog and opened my on-line etsy shop in 2009. Since then I have enjoyed participating in craft fairs and art shows in Canada and the U.S.

I hope people enjoy my jewelry as much as I enjoy making it.

Blog
Etsy Shop

jan avellana is a mixed-media artist with a passion for art making, books, deep conversations, and seaside adventures with her three favorite men (ages 5, 7 and 41). jan spent the better part of her adult life trying very hard to be a grown-up with a traditional job. the birth of her two sons released her to follow her heart and reclaim the artist she has always been. in 2007, jan created a line of silver hand stamped jewelry under the hazelnut cottage brand. today, she revels in mixed-media messes, making heartfelt connections with others through art and words.

in print, you can find jan in "The Pulse of Mixed Media", "Inside the Creative Studio", "Artful Blogging, Winter 2011" and "ClothPaperScissors Studios". in life, you can find her immersed in the studio or at the beach (with paint in her hair). online, you can find jan here:

{etsy shop}
{blog}
{twitter}
{facebook}

Nolwenn Petitbois is a self-taught Mixed Media artist.

Dreamer. Lover. Passionate. Gratitude Warrior. Bookaholic. Cook. Art Journaler...

She came to Mixed Media because she could not decide on only one medium to use in her artwork and it makes her feel more free to experience whatever her heart feels called to.
Nolwenn's artwork usually represents powerful whimsical women (she called them «Nixies») who have a strong positive message to deliver to the Universe, to you. She believes in the strong power of Positive Affirmations and of Gratitude, that both guide her all along in my creative process. She is an eternal learner, and loves to unravel new ways to make her path lighter and stronger. Healing is a huge part of her life path, she is now also a Practical Reiki Master and noticed how it shifted the way it affects her way to do her art.
Nolwenn is also an art journaler and is currently a teacher in the art journaling collaborative playground 21 Secrets that just opened its doors.

Blog
Shoppe
Facebook
YouTube channel
Twitter

Hi! I'm Kelly, the force behind Happy Shack Designs. I live in a happy little shack on the river in Jacksonville, Florida, with my husband and twin daughters. Happy Shack Designs is a dream long in the dreaming. I've wanted to create my own business doing some sort of artwork for as long as I can remember.

Before venturing into my current numerous creative outlets, I spent countless hours working on various needlecraft and sewing projects, skills learned from my mom and my grandmother. I can credit my foray into artisan jewelry to my girls. When they were born, I wanted a mother's bracelet. I saw several styles in catalogs, and all were approximately $100 for a simple double strand. That's when I decided to teach myself how to make jewelry. From there, I was hooked, Happy Shack Designs was born in 2004, and I am self-taught through trial and error.

I'm also a fine art photographer and have loved playing with cameras since I got my first "big girl" camera in the 7th grade. I learned dark room techniques in college but have now fallen in love with all the creative options digital photography brings. My photography often contains layers of texture that add an added dimension to the works.

Lastly, I discovered mixed media and book making in 2009 and have since become addicted to all things paper, paint and stitch! Having a very short attention span serves me well in the variety of art forms I work with.

Outside of my art, I love the outdoors, play the guitar badly, play the piano fairly well, sing somewhere in the middle, love to bake, and have the most adorable red-headed twin daughters ever seen (comin' from a proud Mama); they are the light of my life. I have a bachelor's degree in Communications, a Master's degree in English and work full-time in higher education as the Director of Student Life and Leadership Development (and part time Professor of English!) at a large four-year college in North Florida in addition to my Happy Shack, so it stays pretty crazy in our world most of the time. Oh, yeah, and I'm a little goofy.

Website
Blog
jewelry on Etsy
My art and photos on Etsy
Facebook businesspage
Twitter

Hi there! My name is Robin Norgren and I am a creative entrepreneur. If my life were given a tagline it would be Artist. Writer. Mama. My creative aesthetic is funky. hippie. retro. In 2009 I officially started my first online business called Well of Creations. In 2011, I brought to fruition my second vision which initially started as a blog to highlight Christian artists called My Creative Peace.

In 2012 I decided to begin to integrate my creative business experiences with my educational background. I hold a bachelors degree in business management and worked in retail for more than 20 years before I made the decision in 2000 quit my job and stay home with my newborn babe. I also hold a Master's Degree in theology which I earned while staying home with my girl. All this AND I am a military wife who had the privilege of living through back to back to back deployments from 2008 to 2011 (yep 3 years!). So needless to say I have learned a thing or two about stress management, time management, multitasking and everything in between.

Website
Blog
Facebook
Twitter

Laura Otero is a marketing professional, graphic designer, writer and lover of all things creative living her best life in Charleston, SC. On most days, you will find Laura sharing helpful online tutorials on making the most of the web in between art journaling and photoblogging her latest art endeavor.

 Blogging about online marketing has provided Laura an outlet to share much of what she has learned through her years of experience in the online tourism and advertising markets.

 In fact, as early as 2007, Laura was Facebooking and blogging for her local visitors' bureau (their online fanbase is now well over 40,000 people). She went on to work in online advertising sales for one of South Carolina's most popular NBC television stations, where she sold multi-platform campaigns (including mobile) for a website that served more than 500,000 visitors a month.

Laura enjoys art journaling, painting, making jewelry, traveling and (of course) blogging. She has been known to hold a craft tweet-up and loves handmade items.

Laura chronicles her creative journey towards living an inspired life at lauracatherine.co and shares her online marketing tips and tutorials at marketingwithlaura.com.

I'm Stephanie Guimond, artist, visionary and avid left-brainer. I paint, I dream big and I *love* spreadsheets.

In 2008 I picked up a paint brush for the first time since kindergarten and haven't put it down since. My art, like myself, varies in style and personality from the vintage girly to the unexplainable abstract. The most common theme is visibly the feminine, but I'm always exploring...

Working with materials like acrylics, paper, pastels and ink, I'm drawn to an intuitive and fluid approach to painting where images appear organically before being polished into a finished product. Because of this intuitive nature, pieces are heavily influenced by what I'm living the week, the day or the moment they are created. They reflect a personal story that in an odd way infuses them with a universal quality.

I share my home with hubby and Cassie, our Golden Retriever. I left my 9-5 job last fall to try something different, and spend most of my days working in my guest bedroom turned office/studio creating art and other paid work that supports the life I want to create overall.

Shari Sherman is a Hawaii-born artist/writer who happily makes her home in Florida with her super husband, amazing daughter, 2 big dogs, and 1 black cat. She has been creating all of her life, but it wasn't until her daughter was born that she decided to take being an artist more seriously. "You become defined by what you do, and I wanted my daughter to know me as an artist first."
She considers herself a "fun artist" rather than a fine artist. She is a true multi-media artist making everything from greeting cards to floor cloths. She also illustrated the popular pet sympathy book, Pawprints in Heaven. "That's why I love mixed-media! Painting will always be my first love, but I never want to feel limited in my art. I love photography, words, paper, and jewelry. I want to be able to go wherever my inklings lead me."
No matter the media, bright colors and whimsy are consistent elements of her style. Dogs, mermaids (which she calls Mermies), and anything to do with the beach or ocean are what inspires her. "I make happy art for happy people. That's why I'm here."

Facebook
Blog
Website
Etsy

dani keith has been creating for a lifetime. as a small child she was not intimidated (to her mom's dismay) by the large canvas that was her bedroom wall. this was followed by any surface that was still long enough for her to make her mark. as dani grew, formal classes in drawing, painting, photography and sculpture helped to shape her artistic point of view. in the fall of 2008 she began to flirt with jewelry creation and design. in the spring of 2010 she was set up on a blind date with metals, and she says it was instant, true and deep love at first fuzing! {dk} is constantly evolving, and dani is genuinely excited to see where each turn takes her.

dani holds a BA in Media Studies from UNC-Greensboro, has had the privilege to be mentored by metalsmith Ginger Meek Allen and participated in the life changing course 'flying lessons' by kelly rae roberts

artist statement: "I find the beauty in the simple geometry of shape and transform metal into a story that the wearer wants to be apart of"

Website
Facebook
Twitter
Etsy

Paula Joerling, widely known for her creative use of unorthodox materials in her illustrations, has always been on the cutting edge. She is known for incorporating fabric, stitched paper and found objects into her art.

Forever in search of inspiration, she scours flea markets, antique stores and garage sales in search of goodies to work into her mixed media pieces. Old department store catalogs, vintage wallpaper sample books, costume jewelry and buttons are some favorites. Although she is better known as an illustrator, the sound of paper being stitched has lured her back into the magical world of stitched paper collage and 3 dimensional paper sculptures.

Although she worked for several years as a staff artist for The Lang Companies, primarily she is a freelance artist working with art publishers and licensing companies. Her illustrations are licensed for use on paper goods, table top and gift lines.

Originally from Cincinnati, Ohio, Paula attended the Art Academy of Cincinnati and graduated with a BFA degree in Photography with a minor in Painting. She now lives in Atlanta in a loft with her equally creative husband Tom Haney.

http://www.paulajoerling.com/
https://www.facebook.com/pages/Paula-Joerling-Studio/218183375864

Valerie Weller considers herself an art creator, a lover of color, and a seeker…. She has spent most of her life as a graphic designer with a fine art background, yet in the past few years, has been transitioning into developing & creating her own body of work. Her dream is to create, paint, and share her process full time.

Passionate about color, Valerie works in watercolor, acrylic, oil and mixed media. She holds a BA degree in art with a minor in education. After a solid thirty years of running a successful freelance graphic design business, she is now transitioning to create "part two" of her artistic life, in the world of painting. Currently she is developing various works of art in the mixed media category. From small to large paintings in an organic, intuitive style, to art journaling in watercolor, & mixed media, her work continues to express her passion for color and expressive, organic forms.

Valerie shows her work at boutiques, art shows as well as online through her etsy shop, website, and blog. She is working on an e-course/video series in watercolor, based on the wonderful response to her art journaling pages. Valerie loves to connect with people and works to inspire other's to believe in their own gifts. Her hope is to connect through her art, to cultivate and nurture the development of each person's individual "art spirit".

Etsy shop
Blog
Pinterest

Links:

Blog - http://phyllisdobbs.info/
Website - http://www.phyllisdobbs.com/
Zazzle - http://www.zazzle.com/phyllisdobbs?rf=238522936928369533
Facebook - http://www.facebook.com/pages/Phyllis-Dobbs-Art-Design/171513056197540
Twitter - https://twitter.com/#!/phyllisdobbs

Bio:

Phyllis Dobbs' passion is color and whimsy, both of which she incorporates into her art. Her art is created for licensing on various products, such as fabrics, garden, and gift products. Phyllis' fabric collections, licensed to Quilting Treasures, tie into another love of hers - designing sewing and quilting patterns. She has designed hundreds of quilt and sewing patterns for books and magazines. "Asymmetrical Quilts", published in April, is the latest of 3 quilt books that she has authored.

She began her creative career 25 years ago, by converting her drawings into counted cross stitch, and has never looked back. Always interested in trying new techniques, Phyllis is working on mixed media as well as continuously creating new art, which she guarantees will make you smile.

Originally from Mobile, AL, Phyllis graduated from the University of Alabama with a BS in Interior Design. She continues to take a wide variety of creative and business classes. She lives in Birmingham, AL with her husband and black cat. Phyllis spends most of her time in her studio that feels like a tree house, on the second floor overlooking woods.

Catherine Just is an award winning photographer, motivational speaker, life/business coach and spiritual guide. Her photography has been published on the cover of National Geographic Magazine and inside Oprah.com. She leads Soul*Full Photography Retreats and e-Courses and created the Fear*less movement for people ready to let go of fear and self doubt and embrace their greatness.

You can find out more on her website at
Catherinejust.com

Katie Clemons is a storycatcher.
She helps women capture their memories and document their stories with her eco-friendly journals. Her award-winning business, Gadanke, offers handmade journals filled with writing prompts, European papers, and fun embellishments. She also blogs about simple, handmade living from rural Montana and Berlin, Germany.

celebrate your story.

shop : www.Gadanke.com

blog : www.MakingThisHome.com

Chatting on Facebook: www.facebook.com/Gadanke

I'm Kat Sloma and I'm a photographer, writer and teacher. My online home is in the Kat Eye Studio, where you can join me in my ongoing quest to explore photography, creativity, and inspiration. I love to connect online, sharing my personal creative journey while helping others find their unique vision of the world too.

While I've been studying photography since getting my first film SLR in 2000, it wasn't until 2010 that I declared myself an artist. It took living in Italy for two years on a corporate work assignment to elevate photography from "interest" to "passion." Through capturing images of my extensive travels around Europe along with writing on my blog, The Kat Eye View of the World, I learned the power of images and words together as a form of artistic expression. I found a deeper connection with photography as a revelation of my heart and soul. I discovered that sharing my journey on the blog and through my online courses, I can help others can find the same connection. Could there be anything better to do with my time and energy than empowering others? I don't think so.

I balance my artistic practice and online business with my family and my part-time corporate job as an engineering program manager. It's busy, but I love every minute of it!

Website
Facebook
Twitter
Flickr

A jazzy hello to you! My name is Laura Gaffke and I am passionate about all things positive and living a joyful, meaningful life. I am an artist, teacher, entrepreneur, and a hula girl at heart. I had the pleasure of growing up in New Hampshire where I was fortunate to have the mountains, city and seacoast all within close reach. My diverse surroundings electrified my love of nature and invoked a desire to travel and explore the world. It is from these experiences, as well as my natural ability to focus on the cheerful things in life that my vibrant color palette emerged. I try to engage viewers by revealing intimate, soulful moments from my experiences while working intuitively with paint and collage. It is here where I make meaningful connections.

After graduating from Rivier College with my Bachelor's Degree in both Fine Arts and Art Education I taught in New Hampshire for the next 13 years before moving to Groton, Connecticut and earning my MFA in Interdisciplinary Arts from Goddard College, Vermont. I maintain a dedicated, studio practice in a quaint, old mill building in Westerly, RI where I am an active member of The Artists' Cooperative Gallery in the same town. I also have an online shop, teach, share my work regularly in galleries, contribute to a blog and nurture an ongoing collaborative art practice with a fellow artist, all of which reinforce how connections deeply affect my creative work and life.

"When you do things from your SOUL you feel a river moving in you, a JOY."
~Rumi

WEBSITE: **http://www.lauragaffke.com**
BLOG: http://**lauratwotina.com**
SHOP: **http://www.lauragaffke.etsy.com**
FACEBOOK:**http://www.facebook.com/LauraGaffkeArt**
PINTEREST: **http://pinterest.com/lauragaffke/**
TWITTER: **https://twitter.com/#!/missosally**

My name is Nataša May and I'm an on-line art workshop teacher and a published self taught mixed media artist who paints whimsical pretty faces on layered backgrounds using acrylic paints, color pencils and collage paper to name a few.

Painting is my meditation, my search for answers of the Universe and human existence, my emotional expression and manifestation of my inner thoughts. I tend to gravitate toward whimsical childlike faces as my primary subject or a carrier of the message if you will, but the background begins as an intuitive play with layers of colors.

I'm proud to say my paintings have found their homes all over the world and I hope they are bringing as much joy to their new owners as they have given me through process of painting them.

Blog: http://natashamay.blogspot.com/

You Tube: http://www.youtube.com/playlist?list=PL200F499595287B8A

Facebook: https://www.facebook.com/NatashaMayArtWorld

Pinterest: http://pinterest.com/natasamay/

Julene Ewert grew up in Troy, Idaho, surrounded by a family of artists bursting with creative energy. Her roots are deep in the Palouse, which began with her great-grandmother. Her parents still live on the original homestead and active farm in Troy.

At a young age, Julene knew her destiny was to become an artist. One word of advice from her dad, "Do what you love." With that in mind, she received a Bachelor in Fine Arts with an emphasis in graphic design and advertising from the University of Idaho. She has worked as a designer in Colorado, Washington and Idaho and has clients across the country. In 2006, Julene started her own studio, Present By Design, which has a wonderful product line based on reclaimed items, with a new twist. She also has a whimsical line of greeting cards and mixed-media art prints.

Her artwork can be found in galleries, fine gift stores and homes globally.

Julene finds her passion where she lives in Moscow, Idaho, an undiscovered part of the beautiful Pacific Northwest. Her husband and son give her inspiration and brutally honest critiques.

Artist Statement

Julene Ewert loves to use common materials in surprising new ways.

She loves finding and using bits and pieces of objects from the past.

She dreams of a day when old houses and trees will speak. You can see

influences from her grandma with the use of sewing, quilting and embroidery. Her inspiration comes from nature, travel and everyday life. Her art expresses honesty and tenderness while giving a lighthearted whimsical view—always with rich colors, much like her own spirit. When she starts a piece, the general idea is formed. But what really comes out is something truly remarkable; it is always something that is personal and close to her heart.

website: http://www.presentbydesign.com/

etsy: http://www.etsy.com/shop/presentbydesign

blog: http://blog.presentbydesign.com/

facebook: http://www.facebook.com/pages/Present-by-Design/87038474952

Jodi Lebrun lives in London, OH with her husband Jim, their 4 kids, a Boxer named Kenya and a kitten named Mango. During the week she is a Certified Kaizen-Muse Creativity Coach and Reiki Teacher. On the weekends she enjoys Yoga, painting, puttering in her etsy shop (http://www.etsy.com/shop/creativelifebydesign) growing her own herbs, veggies and all things Divine. She is currently working towards her Master's Degree in spiritual healing through the Reiki Blessings Academy while studying Earth-based Spirituality through Flora Peterson's YAAY program!

Please visit her websites to learn more about her:
www.creativelifebydesign.com
& www.wherethespiritedwomengather.com

About Erin Fickert-Rowland:

Erin Fickert-Rowland is a happy wife, mother of two boys, and Art-lover to the core. She works in multiple mediums, including Oil Painting, Jewelry Design and Mixed Media. She has a degree in Fine Art, with minors in Art History and Philosophy from DePauw University, and has management experience working in Art Galleries, Custom Framing and Custom Home Décor. Erin is currently building and developing her own business, Elysian Studios. Here, she sells her original pieces of Modern Abstract Fine Art and Accessories, and authors a blog about living "The Artful Life." She lives with her family and two dogs just outside of Denver, CO and can frequently be found enjoying the Rocky Mountains- on a bike or snowboard!

Website: www.elysianstudiosart.com
email: erin@elysianstudiosart.com
Facebook: https://www.facebook.com/ElysianStudiosArt
Twitter: https://twitter.com/elysianstudios
Pinterest: http://pinterest.com/elysianstudios/

Louise Gale is the creator of the "Flower of Life Studio" which helps you connect to your true self through creativity, meditation and coaching tools. She also loves to get her hands dirty exploring mixed media techniques and has exhibited her work in New York City with a permanent art collection at the "Hoboken Historical Museum". Louise is currently following her passion to learn all about surface pattern design and exploring the natural patterns we find in our universe. Louise's meditations, kits and e-courses empower others to combine right brain creativity with left brain practical tools, helping to raise the positive energy of individuals
and the world around us.

Links for Louise Gale

Website & blog: http://louisegale.com/
Facebook profile: http://www.facebook.com/louisegaleartist
Facebook page: http://www.facebook.com/LouiseGaleArtandDesign
Twitter: https://twitter.com/LouiseGaleArt

Born into the rustic idyll of central New England, Cindy Silverstein spent her early life steeped in the fields and forests that would imbue her with a lifelong love for the natural world. Whether freelancing as an illustrator for children's book publishers, greeting card companies, or magazines and newspapers, Cindy's gratitude for Earth's simplest gifts flowed through her brush, keeping her grounded. She has worked as art director for difficult-to-please Don Draper types at ad agencies, and has exhibited artwork in galleries in the Northeastern United States. Today, she focuses on mixed media painting and photography, which boast unusually high rates of feline representation.

website/blog: http://creatingartforthespirit.org

Facebook: http://www.facebook.com/CindySilverstein.Artist
Twitter: https://twitter.com/ArtForTheSpirit
Pinterest: http://pinterest.com/csilverstein/

Kim Gann has been painting for over 25 years. Her art and crafts have been sold worldwide. She has created a new collection called Paper Girls which are being offered for the first time here at the Wild Pineapple.

Kim's first creations were wooden-egg Christmas tree ornaments selling from 1986-2009. During those years she also created Driftwood Santa's, Okra Santa's, Wood Slice Art and many other crafts. In 2001 she opened The Crafters Canvas in Lenoir City. She taught art there until 2007. With life changes she closed the doors of her shop but kept the building. During her teaching days Kim never painted for herself, but things changed late one evening in May 2009. Kim nailed two nails into her kitchen wall, hung a 24x36 canvas and a whimsical chicken holding a red coffee cup was born. His name...Cuppa Joe, the father to The Chicken Coop Series.

Kim's love of color shows in the brightly colored paintings where chickens have human characteristics and butterflies dance across the canvas. Her love for old books with the tattered and torn pages finds new life in her latest work Paper Girls. Her art is continually blossoming!

"My goal is to bring joy to the world through my art.
It is a simple prescription for a smile"-KG

off to the studio...

www.kgartstudio.com
www.thechickencoopseries.com
www.facebook.com/thechickencoopseries
www.kimgannart.blogspot.com
http://www.facebook.com/bart.er.98
http://www.linkedin.com/pub/kim-gann/30/7a0/510

Juliette Crane is an artist, teacher, storyteller and adventurer. She spends as much time as possible being inspired by the little things and painting outside, mostly in the grass surrounded by flower gardens and the tallest trees. She's also an avid gardener and enthusiastic cook and would be delighted to have you over for dinner.

She's the creator of a series of online courses that encourage thousands around the world to get creative and live their dreams. From her popular How To Paint An Owl for bird and whimsy-lovers, to the mixed media workshops How To Paint A Girl and How To Create Whimsical Animals for those looking to strengthen their authentic voice and get over their fear of not knowing what to create.

Having fun, learning to let go, and not being afraid to cover up her paintings have become essential to her creative process. She inspires countless individuals with her weekly blog posts, videos and articles, documenting her paintings from start to finish and sharing her life as an artist. She mixes all sorts of materials in her work-acrylics, spray paint, pastels, oils, origami paper, glitter, vintage sheet music and wallpaper.

In the summer of 2009 her sister-in-law gifted her with a few vintage wallpaper books. Juliette fell in love with the colors and patterns and knew she had to do something with the gorgeous paper. So, she remembered what she loved most as a child-cutting out outfits for characters and making up their stories. And that's what started her whimsical paintings. Now she sells the originals and prints around the world and writes books about the process to empower others to share their unique gifts.

Her work has been published in Glamour Magazine UK, Somerset Studio, Somerset Studio Gallery, and Artful Blogging and on blogs including Crescendoh, My Owl Barn and Do What You Love just to name a few.

When she's not teaching, travelling, and painting in gardens around the world, she lives with her bluegrass singing husband in Madison, Wisconsin.

online painting courses: http://juliettecrane.com/workshop/index.shtml

website: http://juliettecrane.com
blog: http://juliettecrane.blogspot.com
twitter: http://twitter.com/juliettecrane
facebook: http://www.facebook.com/JulietteCraneArt

pinterest: http://pinterest.com/juliettecrane/

{jodi}
Jodene Shaw
~Mixed Media Artist/Writer/Photographer/MK Beauty Consultant/Wife/Mom~

"Believe truth. Be real. Be who you are. Don't Blink."
Much of what I create falls into one of those categories.
Four lessons that have changed my life from the inside out . . .that I fight to live out.

~ Believe truth. What I believe is how I will live. So, I might as well believe the truth. I do have to choose to own my truth of here and now. But I'm so glad there is an infinitely bigger, perfect, sacred truth beyond my self. Jesus said, "I am the Way, the Truth, and the Life..." That is where my belief is rooted—about God, about life, about my own identity.

~ **Be real.** Oh, so hard, to be authentic without being pitiful. But my heart dies when I try to paint an image about myself for others to admire or applaud. I have been caught in that snare. So I do my best to stay away from trying to "prove" myself. Life is hard and messy and imperfect, but it still can be great in the midst of all that. I try to find beauty in the inevitable messiness of life. I love this quote from The Velveteen Rabbit, "When you are Real, shabbiness doesn't matter."

~ **Be who you are.** We are made differently with intention and purpose to honor and glorify God. Different is good . . . so, no unfair comparisons to other people! Just be who you were made to be.

~ **Don't blink.** Kenny Chesney cemented this in my mind with his song that I first heard as I was driving our old Chevy ranch pickup moving cattle to our summer pasture. My husband, kids, family, friends, life are all here and now. See them. Enjoy them. Celebrate them and this place where I live on the western prairies: Shaw Ranch, White Owl, South Dakota, which has distinct beauty to delight, to savor. Beauty right here, right now, wherever I am. Don't blink, really see it.

BLOG "Opened Door": www.jodeneshaw.blogspot.com
Art Shop: www.etsy.com/Shop/JodeneShaw
Find me on Facebook: Jodene Shaw, Mixed Media Art & Photography
Mary Kay Shop online 24/7: www.marykay.com/jshaw2
Email: jshaw2@marykay.com or jjtsshaw@gwtc.net

Carrie Schmitt began painting after developing a life-threatening allergy to heat in 2009. While stuck inside for the entire summer due to the heat in Cincinnati, she pursued her dream to become an artist, picked up a paintbrush and began experimenting.

Since then, her family has moved to the Pacific Northwest to enjoy a more temperate climate, and she now paints on a daily basis in her studio as a full-time artist. Her artwork begins with inspiration from flowers and the natural world.

"Starting with the organic shapes and color palettes found in nature, I let my paintings emerge and reveal themselves over time and layers of paint," she says. "I'm delighted by the intersection of color and form, as well as the juxtaposition of balance and the unexpected."

In addition to sharing her creative process, she shares her favorite home décor projects and vintage finds on her blog.

My website is: www.carrieschmittdesign.com
Facebook: www.faceboook.com/carrieschmittartanddesign
Pinterest: http://pinterest.com/carrieart/

Valerie Hart is an artist, designer, writer and day dreamer. Her passion to create art started as a child and she dreamed of being an artist since grade school, where she had the dubious title of class artist. Her mother was always telling her to "get her head out of the clouds", which incidentally made her wonder even more. Though Valerie studied art and graphic design in college, she ended up with a responsible degree in business.

After graduation and with her head firmly in the clouds, she got her first job at a small publishing company as a graphic artist. This auspicious start led to a corporate career in advertising and marketing as a graphic designer, art director and creative director. Finally, the day came when she wanted to create her own art and designs. So she dusted off her paints and brushes and began. Out came the wonderfully whimsical cats, sheep, mermaids, girls and frog illustrations you see today. Her art and designs are inspired by color, nature and her imagination.

In 2011, Valerie set her sites on the licensing market for her art and designs. She continues to work on her whimsical illustrations and unique designs building her up her portfolio of work. She lives in beautiful New England, creating from her home studio with her two furry companions, Bella, a tortie cat and Lily, a lab mix.

https://www.facebook.com/valeriehartstudio

https://twitter.com/valhartdesign
http://pinterest.com/valeriehart
http://www.flickr.com/photos/valeriehart
http://www.etsy.com/shop/valeriehartstudio

Elizabeth Gonzalez

I have loved the process of creating since I was a child. My mom and my aunt taught me crochet when I was nine. Later I learned sewing, needlepoint, embroidery, papier mache, glass work, ceramics and recently painting and collage. I began my journey in the art business in 1996 after a ceramic workshop. From that moment my imagination began to fly. I learned in that workshop that I could transform that clay in almost anything I wanted. I started with some butterflies (still making them), photo frames and welcome plates. I took some of those to a lovely store in my home town and I started selling right there. After that experience, my life made a huge turn. From an Industrial Engineer and professor of management to a creative life in ceramics. My work in ceramic is hand built with clay slabs, fired to a very high temperature, painted with slips, stains, under glazes and glazes and fired again to a very high temperature. After 12 years in ceramics I gave a try on mixed media in 2009 and I it was "love at first sight"(or first try?). I spend most of my time creating art (in my mind) and drawing icons that can inspire my work in ceramic and mixed media. I love creating mixed media art using collage and journalism with papers painted and design by me. Adding meaningful details to my collages is my passion. I have added my new found passion for surface pattern to my mixed media, too. I draw icons and paint them to be used as a pattern or a detail to my mixed media. I find great pleasure in adding ceramic details to my mixed media work, too. You will find a tiny flower, a heart, a leave or a word in almost all my mixed media art and in the ceramic art, too. This is the way I express my feelings and my desire to inspire others to live a lovely life and enjoy the process. I love to make people smile with my art; this is a mission I have embraced since I learned it from a client a long time ago. My mission..."makes art that makes you smile and feel inspire to live a peaceful and lovely life "enjoying the ride...through this amazing life".
I love the idea that my art is around the world since it is sold in very important stores in Puerto Rico where tourists buy. If you come to Puerto Rico you could find my art in the Old San Juan at Puerto Rico Arts & Crafts Store in Fortaleza Street. If you get to visit the Museum of Art of Puerto Rico, go and visit the lovely store which sells art from amazing artists living in Puerto Rico as well as mine. I know you will enjoy that visit a lot.
My designs are always inspired by a truly passion for nature and family life. My

creations adorned many homes in Puerto Rico and around the world in countries such as Argentina, Brazil, Costa Rica, United States, Hungary, India, Italy, among others.

I have a very big family with seven sisters and five brothers and also blessed with three sons, Gabriel, Cristian, and Víctor André; a lovely grandson, Javier André; two great daughters in law, Anyelis and Sheynel and my first granddaughter, Aliany Gabriela.

Thanks for visiting and "Enjoy the Ride"

http://elizabethglz.com

http://www.flickr.com/photos/elizabethglz/

https://twitter.com/elizabethglz

https://www.facebook.com/pages/Elizabeth-GLZ/108106265903520

http://pinterest.com/eglzpin/

http://elizabethglz.etsy.com

Offerings:
E-Course

http://elizabethglz.com/register

Lisa Renee Wilson is an Awareness Artist, exploring the relationship between mindfulness, creativity, and the stuff of *Real Life*.

She writes regularly at LifeUnity.com and guides others in a variety of creative expression and self-awareness classes online. (Learn more about these classes at the website listed below!) Lisa also creates encaustic and mixed-media art in her home studio area in Bloomington, IN, where she lives with her husband and two children.

Find Lisa online here:

Website: http://www.lifeunity.com
Facebook (personal page): http://www.facebook.com/lisareneewilson
Facebook (LifeUnity) http://www.facebook.com/lifeunity
Twitter: http://www.twitter.com/lifeunity

e'Layne Koenigsberg is a mixed media collage artist, business owner, artist empowerment coach, author, teacher and mother. Her mission is to create inspirational art and to empower women to thrive spiritually, emotionally, artistically and financially.

Some of e'Layne's first and fondest memories were designing clothes with her nana at age four. Drawing her poodle was a passion. Growing up e'Layne and her mother took many crafty classes together. Her hands were always busy.

When she started college majoring in art the teacher in her first class instructed the students to draw an egg. e'Layne informed the teacher she wasn't inspired to draw an egg and he assured her she was in the wrong class. It was that day her creative spirit was squelched and she became a sociology major.

It took a spiritual quest to regain her desire, inspiration and confidence to explore art and to get in touch with her creative spirit…months camping in Shenandoah National Park, mime school in Boulder, Colorado and zig zagging across America in a Volkswagen camper. e'Layne's journey took her from living in Florida most of her life to landing in Orinda, California where she attended graduate school at John F. Kennedy University. Majoring in the field of Transpersonal Counseling Psychology and studying Jungian dream work and ancient visual symbols began to re-awaken the artist and wild woman within. Photography was also food for her soul.

Over twenty-five years ago love took e'Layne from California to Maui, Hawaii, where she began her business, "Gypsy In Me," selling hand-painted clothing and designing jewelry. In addition to traveling the art show circuit for more than two decades, in 1996, she co-founded an art gallery called Wild Women Gallery. Presently, e'Layne calls two places home. In Tallahassee, Florida, she manages a thriving artist community called Railroad Square Art Park. On St. Pete Beach, she lives with her partner and they run a fantastic art business…3 Hip Chics…the production wing of Art by e'Layne. You can also find e'Layne's art and articles in many Stampington Publication magazines.

www.artbyelayne.com
www.facebook.com/artbyelayne
www.twitter.com/ArtbyElayne
www.linkedin.com/in/elaynekoenigsberg

pinterest.com/elayne/

Mary C. Nasser earned her Master of Fine Arts in Studio Art. In 1996 she was a visiting artist and guest lecturer in Cluj-Napoca, Romania, where she lectured at Academia de Arte Vizuale "IOAN ANDREESCU" (Academy of Visual Arts) and exhibited her work in "Deschideti U.S.A." (Open the Door) at the Casa Matei. Mary has had more than 20 solo shows in the past 10 years and has been awarded numerous residency opportunities. She was Artist-in-Residence in 2008 at Red Cinder Creativity Center in Hawaii, where she lived near active volcanoes that continually recreate the landscape and studied the various landscapes and dynamic geology of the island. The dramatic volcanic landscapes continue to inform and influence her artwork. Her latest residency was at Osage Arts Community in Missouri.

In 2010, a jury selected Mary's sculpture proposal for Wings in the City – a project to raise funds for the Jennifer and Jim Koman Expressive Therapy Program at Wings, a BJC pediatric hospice and palliative care program. Mary's 5-foot by 4-foot fiberglass butterfly sculpture is entitled *Journey* and is sponsored by Plaza Mercedes Benz. It is embellished with metallic acrylics and maps, much like her recent paintings. The butterflies were auctioned off May 21, 2011, at Wings in the City's *Art Takes Flight* auction. The public art project raised $1.3 million dollars for BJC's pediatric hospice program Wings.

Throughout the year, Mary leads *Garden Art* (Art Therapy) activities at St. Louis Children's Hospital and *Healing Through the Arts* art therapy workshops for both children and adults at St. John's Mercy Medical Center.

She is represented by Wood Icing Studio & Gallery, Edwardsville Arts Center, Sole Survivor Art Gallery, Lillian Yahn Gallery, Artlandish Gallery, and The Little Gallery at Art Saint Louis.

Website: www.marycnasser.com
Blog: www.marycnasser.com/blog
Shop: http://www.etsy.com/shop/marycnasser
Facebook: www.facebook.com/MaryNasserArt
Twitter: www.twitter.com/marycnasser
Pinterest: http://pinterest.com/marycnasser

Amanda Fall is a joy-seeker and art-maker, blessed beyond belief to create and edit Sprout online magazine. She invites you on a mission to color the world, to seek beauty in the mundane, to practice gratitude, and to celebrate abundant joy in this divinely blessed life. Join the conversation on Facebook, in the pages of Sprout, and at her personal blog Persistent Green.

My name is Beth Doan. I am an Artist and I live and work on the beautiful coast of Maine! I'm Administrative Assistant for the Town of Camden by day and an Artist by night! Although, in reality, I rise early most every morning and begin my day with a lovely cup of coffee and paint for the first couple of hours of day. It is important and vital to my well being to put creativity as my first priority as much as possible.

I am a traditional and decorative artist. And I have just begun dabbling with photography and mixed media art. I also love to create jewelry, sew, knit, and crochet.

I love to paint on wooden surfaces, particularly mini Lobster Buoys. My best experiences creatively, hands down, have been from custom order requests to personalize them for Weddings, Anniversaries & Showers. Getting to know the bride or customer planning the event is very satisfying and meaningful.
My next favorite surface to paint on is glass ornaments and then anything I can harvest from the sea. Sometimes I find it hard to fall asleep at night because my brain is so busy creating my next project.

Some of my favorite themes to paint are lupines, lighthouses, blueberries, lobsters, dragonflies, snowmen and flowers. But having said that, I'm always trying something new. I love a creative challenge. I love the feelings I get when I create something special for someone else.

I am also a proud member and leader of the Etsy Maine Team.

www.bethscraftroom.etsy.com
http://www.facebook.com/MaineTeam
http://bethscraftroom.blogspot.com/
http://www.facebook.com/pages/Beth-Doan/

Katherine Quinn is the short, curly haired, New Zealand artist behind Sleep and her Sisters. She works part time from her kitchen table in the sunny Hawke's Bay where she likes watching clouds, buying apple flavored lollies and often thinks about the day she had lunch in Paris.

She loves to create with pretty much anything that she can make a mark with, but her most favorite materials are water colour pencils, acrylic paint and collaging.

She has recently discovered the world of surface pattern design and has fallen completely head over heels in love with multiplying everything {except mushrooms, she's not so fond of them}.

Facebook: www.facebook.com/pages/Sleep-and-her-Sisters/109447779084636
Website: www.sleepandhersisters.co.nz/
Twitter: twitter.com/katherineq
Pinterest: pinterest.com/katherinequinn/
Flickr: http://www.flickr.com/photos/sleepandhersisters/

Liv Lane calls herself a Human Sparkler, dedicated to helping women and youth illuminate and celebrate their passions and sense of purpose. Liv follows her bliss by teaching e-courses for soulful entrepreneurs {including her newest offering, BuzzWorthy}, writing and speaking about finding your spark, creating inspirational art, and blogging about it all. Liv lives in a suburb of Minneapolis with her husband, two young boys, one crazy dog, and an army of invisible angels. Find her online at LivLane.com and follow her Choosing Beauty blog.

Mandy Saile (a.k.a. "Bijou" of 'Bijou's Whimsy') was born in 1977, in North Bay, Ontario, Canada. She can't remember a time when a pencil was not a constant companion so it was no surprise that she was off to art college at a very young age. She just knew early on that she was destined to be a visual communicator. She describes herself as a creative & inspired maker of whimsical things. She is a woman who's usually most comfortable around animals, or in rooms full of books. She is a self-confessed rabbit addict and naturally a vegetarian and animal advocate. She's had a long standing dream of opening her own rabbit sanctuary/rescue & one of her biggest wishes is to see a worldwide ban on animal testing & for the seal hunt to end. Mandy's creative journey however is plagued by severe chronic & acute migraines, but tries not to let them slow her down too much.

She graduated from the Ontario College of Art & Design with associate & honors standing in 1999, where she minored in communication & design and majored in illustration. After several years in the big city Mandy headed back to the North where she currently makes her home/warren amongst the trees and fresh air of her beloved North Bay, alongside her honey, Jonathan and their little family of rabbits. Mandy has been a full-time artist for several years now and she feels ever so blessed to be able to make artwork to her hearts content whiles surrounded by sweet rabbit souls, it is a dream come true for her.

Mandy loves to create work that takes people away from their present even if but momentarily. She tries to create images that refresh the soul and fill the viewer with joy. She aspires to simply inspire and shed a bit of light & colour in a world that is often quite dark and ultimately she is driven to create artwork with a strong message of connection and kindness. She hopes that her work will prompt reflection and thought and bring attention to the beauty of animals, their plight and the need for their conservation. Her captivating imagery has a unique, vibrant and whimsical style and using a sophisticated colour palette She also wants to share her love of colour and thrill the viewer with her palette whiles creating images infused with heart, thought, & positive energy. Living a creative, joyful and inspired life is a priority for this artist.

Her inspiration comes from a myriad of things including: music, literature, dreams, spirituality, psychology and the strength of the human spirit. But, usually, her main inspiration comes from animals & the relationship/kinship between humans & the natural environment. Mandy finds so much joy and beauty in nature and in its unique inhabitants and tries to infuse the love, respect, awe & inspiration she feels for the natural world with almost every piece she creates.

Mandy offers her unique illustrations & creations as prints in her online shops. She applies her imagery to greeting cards & jewelry, as well as a myriad of other whimsical handmade goodies.   She hopes you'll find time to hop over to her blog & website for a visit...and don't be shy to say hello or ask questions.

Links:
Portfolio: **www.BijousWhimsy.com**
Blog: **www.BijousWhimsy.Blogspot.com**
Online Shop: **www.BijousWhimsy.Etsy.com**
Email: **MandySaile@BijousWhimsy.com**

About the Author:

Robin Norgren
Life Coach/Creativity Teacher/ Author
Located in Arizona

I create heart opening programs that utilize your Creativity and your Faith in God to navigate through the trials of life.

My life, my story, my relationship with God is not simply meant to encourage other Jesus followers; it is to reach whoever is looking for TOOLS AND STRATEGIES to live more fully.

I strive to live life to the fullest. No matter what. I have grown into myself through my love for Jesus and HIS LOVE FOR ME. Art, motherhood, business, creativity and yoga are the cherished vehicles for this deepening.

Life can be
FULL, JUICY, MEANINGFUL, PURPOSE FILLED, LOVELY

I want to help you come to your fullest life. I create workbooks, e-courses and workshops that chronicle my change and growth and offer you ways to find out what
YOUR FULLEST life
will be.

My passion for life coaching...

What brings me to life coaching? What a huge question! For the first time in my life I feel like I am doing the exact right thing at the exact right time. My background is in business and in theology. The 'plan" was to join the military and become a chaplain. But many obstacles and life changes had caused me for the last 5 years to wonder how could I have been so wrong about the direction I was going to go. Then I began co-facilitating support groups and was actually "fired" from volunteer positions over my style and the way I wanted to come alongside people. My "style" were dismissed as "inappropriate" for those types of group settings.

So one day in 2012 I SUDDENLY remembered a suggestion 10 years ago from a friend that I should consider life coaching. And I thought, why not? From the very moment I began reading the material, I realized THIS is what I was trying to do but it was in groups that were geared more towards therapy. Then I came to week 1 of my first module in my certification and what was the subject:

THE ART OF QUESTIONING

Anyone who knows me knows that I love to ask questions and truly believe that the right question asked at the right time can change a person.

Find me in Kindle under "Robin Norgren"

Education:
Life Coach Certification, Southwest Institute of Healing Arts, 2012
Masters of Theology, Fuller Theological Seminary, 2007
Bachelor of Science, Business Arizona State University, 2000

Certifications:
C-YT 200 Hour, Holy Yoga, 2008
Facilitator, Mending the Soul, 2009
Flying Lessons, Kelly Rae Roberts Business Course, 2010
Hello Soul Hello Business, Kelly Rae Roberts/Beth Nicholls, 2012
The Spark Kit, Danielle LaPorte, 2012

Social Media Links:

Websites:
http://www.robinnorgren.com
http://www.mycreativepeace.com

Twitter: http://www.twitter.com/robinlnorgren
Youtube: http://www.youtube.com/wellofcreations
Facebook: http://www.facebook.com/robinnorgrenstudios
Pinterest: http://www.pinterest/robinnorgren

www.ingramcontent.com/pod-product-compliance
Lightning Source LLC
Chambersburg PA
CBHW051627170526
45167CB00001B/92